AMERICA
What Happened?

DOUGLAS DICKENSON

ISBN: 978-1-64516-511-8   (Paperback Edition)
ISBN: 978-1-64516-510-1   (Hardcover Edition)
ISBN: 978-1-64516-512-5   (E-book Edition)

Book Ordering Information

Phone Number: 347-901-4929 or 347-901-4920
Email: info@globalsummithouse.com
Global Summit House
www.globalsummithouse.com

Printed in the United States of America

CONTENTS

America What Happened?

When writing this book, the many problems that exist in our country that should have been addressed by the presidents and congress over many years were not. When they all campaigned for office they talked about the problems and sounded like they were going to do something about them; but after taking office they did nothing and even the talk ended. A recent example is Bush, Clinton and Obama when campaigning for office said Jerusalem should be the capital of the Jews but never made it happen; they wanted the Jewish vote to get elected but not the backlash from other countries; the same is true for our other problems. I'm talking about illegal immigration and our borders, NAFTA and AFTA draining our money and our jobs, term limits, Social Security, taxes and more.

When I say no one has done anything about these, I mean both major political parties going back decades.

It was depressing to see these problems looming even worse in the future with little hope anyone would try to fix them.

Who would have ever thought that a man who had never run for office of any kind would decide to run for the highest office in the country and against Hillary Clinton who was predicted by all of the pollsters to be the next President.

President Trump is addressing many of the issues that all Americans should be concerned about; it is obvious to the casual observer that he wasn't like the professional politicians but ran for office because he recognized the many problems and wanted to fix them because he cares about our country and the people. He has taken on a job that the establishment does not support; it is an uphill battle with little support from his own party and absolutely no support from the Democrats. Much of what he has corrected came from executive orders. He needs the support of the people getting involved and calling and writing their congressman demanding they start working with the president instead of against him.

Introduction

I was born in 1939 and lived through WW2, Korean War, Vietnam and all the others that followed. My observations and suggestions are not out of a book written for the classroom to indoctrinate the young, but are based on decades of experience. I grew up in Flint Michigan in a blue collar family; my grandfather started to work for Buick in 1914 and my father with Fisher Body in 1928. I became one of a very few white collar workers in my family. My family did not attend church and religion was almost never discussed so my religious beliefs did not come from my upbringing but from observing the history of the world and observing the operation and practices of most of the main line Christian churches. As early as 12 years old I started searching religions trying to find out about God. I attended Baptist, Methodist, Nazarene, Mormon, and The church of latter day saints when God finally revealed himself to me.

Since my family were all blue-collar auto workers, they were all registered Democrats. I started out voting for John F Kennedy but as the Democrat Party started to turn away from the ideas and beliefs of President Kennedy, I moved closer to the Republican Party which also started to change and now consider myself an Independent where I can choose the person running for office based on their beliefs regardless of party affiliation.

I started to work for IBM in 1965; this was the beginning of the computer age and IBM was just starting to ship the 360 computer systems for business use; the personal computer had not been developed yet. It was exciting to be involved in the leading-edge of the boom in technology and our country was prospering.

It doesn't matter if you are an Independent, Republican or Democrat you must know our country is in terrible shape and what's worse, our politicians and most of the media do not let us know how bad it is; they certainly offer little in the way of solutions and whatever solutions they do offer I can't believe will fix anything. If the politicians keep procrastinating, the problems will overwhelm us. We can't just blame the politicians because we elect them and set back and allow them to make bad decisions and never get involved to reverse them until the damage is done. It is my hope that my book will help you to understand the problems we face with some ideas of what it will take to get us back on the right track. Keep in mind we have waited so long, the solutions will not be easy, but if we continue to keep our head buried in the sand, the solutions will be even worse.

Humpty-Dumpty sat on a wall,
Humpty-Dumpty had a great fall;
All the king's horses and all
The King's men,
Couldn't put Humpty-Dumpty
Together again.

As a very young child I learned such rhymes as, Mary Mary quite contrary, little Bo peep, little Jack Horner, Jack and Jill, Mary had a little lamb, and many more. To a child they were just cute little rhymes and nothing more, but in reality, many of them were political in nature. Mary Mary quite contrary referred to Mary 1 of England who was called Bloody Mary for her persecuting and murdering many Protestants. Jack and Jill were about King Louis XVI who was beheaded and Queen Marie Antoinette who came tumbling after.

Humpty-Dumpty was a cannon mounted on top of the ST. Mary's at the wall church in Colchester England. During a siege of the church during the English Civil War in 1648, the tower was hit and the cannon Humpty-Dumpty fell to the ground. The King's men on horses tried to retrieve the cannon to no avail

Humpty-Dumpty appeared in a Mother Goose story book in 1902 as a riddle with the answer being "an egg" It's obvious we can make Humpty-Dumpty anything we want it to represent. To me it represents a fall that the results are difficult if not impossible to fix.

I see Humpty-Dumpty as America! We have been sitting high up on the wall since God blessed us with a land of milk and honey for the gentiles. We have had our ups and downs over the years just as the Jews did in the land of Canaan, but finally God grew weary of their sin and rebellion. It's true that God loves us; (us being the gentiles), but it's also true that his anger can easily match his love.

I believe the people in the United States, just like the Jews (the chosen people) have become so sinful and rebellious, that we are about to reach a time with God where he removes his helping hand and out fate will be the same as the Jews, or even worse? I'm not picking on the Jews, just using their plight as described in the Old Testament to compare to ours to show that when all is said and done, there isn't really any basic difference between peoples.

Are we about to fall off our perch and break apart just like Humpty-Dumpty in the children's nursery rhyme? Remember, the entire King's horses and all the King's men; but we don't have a King; perhaps, all the President's Senators and all the President's Congressmen couldn't put America together again. Did I forget their advisors?

The Jews were given a land of milk and honey by God because they were the chosen people of the time; they weren't perfect as no one is, but compared to the other people in the world at that time; they were the best. For those of us that are familiar with the Old Testament, we know they fell away from God and he removed his hand from the twelve tribes of Israel. Life deteriorated and their enemies defeated them. The Israelites would repent and God would restore them to grace and power.

Every time they turned their back on God who had blessed their lives greatly; their punishment would get worse. God decided, (to what I believe is mankind's last chance); to give his son Jesus as a sacrifice; so that all that would believe in him, repent of their sins, and follow him would be indwelled with the Holy Spirit, and capable of living a righteous life; he then left us without excuse!

Israel for the most part, rejected Jesus as the Messiah mentioned in their Old Testament In spite of his teachings and the many miracles he performed. Since they were occupied by the Romans, they may have convinced themselves that the Messiah would free them and restore Israel to power and influence it once had enjoyed. It was about 35 years following the crucifixion that the Jews rose up against the Romans and were easily defeated. The Romans burned their temple to the ground. About 70 years later they again attempted to defeat the Romans and this time they were banned from Jerusalem and from worshiping their God.

Over the centuries, the Jews are driven out of many countries in Europe; they were blamed for every disaster from the plague to worldwide depression; this was the Diaspora of the once great nation. For almost 1800 years, the Jews no longer had a country. Following WWII, when it was reported that several million Jews had been killed in the holocaust; the allies decided to give the Jews a homeland which is where they reside today. The Jews have really never known peace following the crucifixion of Jesus, even to this day as they are surrounded by nations that hate them and would like to destroy them completely. I wonder if the Jews that don't believe that Jesus was the messiah as written in the book of Danial some 500 years before Christ; how can they explain that 2000 years later and there is no Messiah? Perhaps they were mistaken and need to rethink their position.

When I wrote this book four years ago, Donald Trump had not decided to run for president now that he is president, and is addressing some of the major issues in my book, I felt a need to provide an update as things are starting to look up There actually may be hope for the United States. Could there be a light at the end of the tunnel?

Chapter 1

America, another Land of Milk and Honey

America enters the scene in a land; that, I believe is a land of milk and honey provided by God for the Christians. Oh, if you're not a Christian, don't worry, you still get to reap the benefits. It's not that there weren't Christians in Europe, but the practice of Christianity was not what it should be. Many of our early immigrants were escaping religious persecution in Europe. This was the opportunity to establish a Judeo-Christian country that provided religious freedom. We were the example to the world in the way we lived our lives. We were the most respected, feared, admired and successful country on the earth.

Our ancestors came to a new world that was wild and unsettled. Many died from disease and starvation but in spite of the hardships, a nation started to form; a nation that would be different from any nation on earth.

We take for granted where we are today; how far we have come in such a relatively short time when you consider that European countries had existed for many centuries when we were just beginning.

Europe was already well established when we decided to break away from European control and influence and start over; while rejecting many of their ways. The United States was just getting started but it was not long before we passed them by. Some would consider this bragging but it's not; just a fact that is obvious to the whole world.

President Theodore Roosevelt once told a reporter "The world will never love us, they may respect us, they might one day fear us, but they will never love us, for we have too much audacity". The dictionary describes audacity as, brazen, insolent. I believe we are what Roosevelt described and that's part of why we were so driven that success quickly followed.

I have always believed the two main reasons America became such a unique and unusual country is; first, the immigrants that would come to such an undeveloped land and leave everything they knew, country, family and friends, had to be quite unique themselves. I do not compare these to the illegal immigrants crossing our borders as they are coming to an established country to make more money.

The second reason for our success is we were able to keep the best ideas and traditions of the various nations while rejecting their worse. This was only possible because we were not a country of one nationality, but a melting pot of the world. The result was a society different from the rest of the world.

Perhaps the best example of this difference between America and most of the established countries was our ultimate approach to religious freedom. Most countries had one or two main religions and in some cases a person would be persecuted if they failed to endorse the state religion

As I said, it is human nature to take for granted what we have, and how we got there. When you look at our accomplishments in just 242 years, it's really quite amazing! We are a leader in medicine, inventions, technology and space travel just to name a few. No other nation on earth has ever reached the lever of achievement of America, and it was all accomplished by a melting pot of peoples from every country in the world.

Because of how our forefathers founded our country combined with the kind of people that immigrated here looking for a better life, we enjoy an exceptional standard of living; not only do we have one of the largest per capita incomes, but our cost of living is much lower than Europe's.

One of the main reasons Europe has such a high cost of living is Taxes. Most of the European countries operate under socialism, which has the goal of giving everyone the same standard of living. This would be accomplished by income redistribution, or, take from those that have and give to those who do not. Now financial equality has never actually been accomplished in any country; what I see is the entire middle class living at a level below America's lower class while the privileged upper class still exists, and the government makes most decisions instead of the people and free enterprise...

A good example of the government making decisions to control your life is in France, they buy gasoline at the same price as in the United States but the government doesn't want people to drive so they place a tax that accounts for about 57 percent of the cost of gas while in our country, the total tax both federal and state average just 11 percent. At the current time, gas in the United States is about $2.57 a gallon while in Europe it averages about $7.84 and they are protesting in the streets over the cost but the people put socialist in power so from my perspective they are protesting against themselves.

Speaking of taxes; Finland in Europe has a 20% value added tax which means if they buy a $40.000 auto, they pay $8.000 tax. We know a couple that fly to the United States, buy the same car and ship it home and they save thousands; so that's exactly what they do.

Are you aware that a value added tax was one of the options being considered by the Obama administration to help pay off the debt? A value added tax on top of Federal income tax and State income tax and sales tax and property tax and gasoline tax and luxury tax and on and on go the ways government has to take your money and lower your standard of living.

Do you remember reading about how our forefathers threw the tea in the Boston harbor to protest, taxation without representation?

Socialist societies have high taxation with representation; perhaps because they're looking for their government to take care of them instead of taking care of themselves and they are willing to live at a much lower standard of living. While they may be willing to have less, it's unfortunately human nature to be jealous or resentful of those that have more and many socialist countries feel that way about Americans.

If the Obama administration was successful in establishing socialist programs; president Obama may have accomplished his goal of making the rest of the world love us, because we would be living at the same level as they are.

I certainly can't speak for the American people, but for me, I would just as soon tolerate their resentment and keep my standard of living and live in a country where if I'm willing to work hard and make sacrifices, I can achieve my goals; not the goals of the political establishment.

My wife and I spent a month in France in the summer of 1990. I was sent there by my company as part of a team to resolve a computer problem they were having. This particular computer product had been developed at their lab which was located just outside of Nice, which is located on the French Rivera. My wife of course, fearing that I would be lonely without her, decided to go with me. It's amazing the sacrifices a wife is willing to make for her husband. While I worked during the day, my wife would handle all the shopping and sightseeing that I was not able to do; did I mention earlier a wife's sacrifice?

Each weekend we would travel to various locations which included Italy, Austria, Switzerland and other cities in France including Paris. To ensure you had your own bathroom, you needed to book a room in a four star hotel. Some three star hotels required you to share a bathroom with other rooms. The room at a four star hotel was much smaller than any room at the least expensive American motel chain, while the price was double that of a mid price hotel chain in our country.

At a restaurant, you don't get ice in your drink unless you pay extra and the food prices are high. The quantity of food is about half of what is served in an American restaurant which is one reason Europeans are less prone to obesity. It would be a good idea in this case, if we would emulate Europe and reduce our serving sizes. It would help us control our weight while saving money; the point is a small amount of food for a very high price. Beside the small meals, Europeans walk many places because not all have automobiles and the price of gas is about 2.5 times the US rate.

My wife and I traveled one weekend from Nice to Florence Italy, then to Pizza and back to Nice; the trip covered about 450 miles and we traveled the autostrade which is like the autobahn in Germany. Both of these are like our interstates. If you ever traveled our interstate highways you know how heavy the traffic is; well the autostrade was almost empty. Once in awhile a BMW or some other fast car would pass at a high rate of speed but the average person didn't travel the autostrade because the cost of the tolls was about $77.00 to travel 450 miles and with gas in 1990 about $5.00 per gallon.

Mopeds and bicycles are much more common in Europe because that's the way most people can afford to travel. France has an average of one car per 2.5 people while the United States averages 2.28 cars per household.

You can see that comparing the per capita income between Europe and the United States doesn't tell the whole story because when you factor in the cost of living, our standard of living far exceeds Europe's.

It's not hard to see why a person might feel that the United States from its very inception was a land that God blessed, hoping that unlike the chosen people from the Old Testament, Christians would love him enough to keep his words; and he in turn would continue to bless us.

Chapter 2

The Roaring 20's

America started a rebellious time in the 1920's. World War1 had ended in November 1918. It was a terrible bloody war especially when compared to modern warfare. The United States had 116,000 military deaths and 205,000 wounded. The total casualties of World War One were 37 million; 16 million dead and 21 million wounded. Of the dead, 9.7 million were military and 6.8 million were civilian.

Now that the war had ended and life returning to normal, congress responding to pressure from the Temperance Movement, passed the 18th amendment to the constitution which prohibited the manufacture and sale of alcoholic beverages. The amendment passed in January 1919 to take effect in January 1920.

Prohibition ended in December 1933 when the 21st amendment to the constitution was passed which effectively canceled the 18th amendment. The 18th amendment was a case where not only congress but the 36 state legislatures required amending the constitution, failed to look at the reality of such a law and the subsequent results.

Hidden breweries were raided and the equipment destroyed. Stills where illegal whisky was brewed were hidden in the woods. Federal agents searched for them and some never returned. The exact number of Federal agents killed is not available but the figure is estimated at several hundred.

I had heard as a young man that in the Ozarks of Arkansas, revenuers, as the federal agents were referred to, pretty much quit trying to enforce prohibition and the tax law. When prohibition ended in 1933, the manufacture of illegal whisky did not, because the government imposed heavy taxes on liquor.

I had always thought that bootleggers referred to the people that made the whisky but it was actually more about the drivers that delivered it. Bootlegging was the term used to describe a maneuver where the driver when being pursued by revenuers, would turn the wheel without hitting the brake and reverse direction to escape their pursuers. The bootleggers were skilled drivers and because of their skill were often able to escape. The bootleggers are credited with starting NASCAR and it's reported some of the early drivers became rich running booze. Today's movies often use the bootleg procedure to reverse direction during car chases.

It is reported that the first year of prohibition, Americans consumed more alcohol than ever before. People began making bathtub booze and some was bad and blindness and death occurred. The Mob became rich during prohibition years by running booze, prostitution and gambling. Speakeasies popped up all over the country and the Federal Government lost a huge amount of tax money. I don't think this was the results those that endorsed prohibition were hoping for.

There were twice as many speakeasies during prohibition as there were legal bars previously. People had lost respect for the law because they were trying to force their version of morality on everyone. I'm sure it was exciting going to the illegal speakeasies and when we have an issue that we disagree on, it becomes easier to rebel against other issues of morality.

Gangsters provided most of the booze to the speakeasies and the general public knew it but it didn't stop them from frequenting those places. They also had to know that the gangsters were involved with drugs, prostitution, gambling, even murder.

The women were partying and drinking as never before wearing skimpy dresses while they danced to the Charleston. This was the good life! It reminds me of that beer commercial; "it doesn't get any better than this".

The stock market was on the rise and you could buy stock on margin Buying on margin meant you could buy $10,000 worth of stock for only $1,000 down; if the value of the stock went up to $11,000, you doubled your $1,000 investment. The risky down side of buying on margin; if the stock dropped to $9,000 you had to make up the $1,000 loss or lose the stock; times were so good, why worry, this could never happen.

Consumer debt was high and banks were making overoptimistic loans. Wow! Does this scenario sound familiar? Do we never learn? When you look at history, you will find that previous societies never seemed to learn from other's mistakes, or even their own. I don't know who coined the phrase "once bit twice shy", but it doesn't appear to apply to most of life; especially if it's been awhile since bit.

Well we all know the ending to this story; the market dropped 25% on black Friday and just about everyone lost their entire investment. Former multimillionaires were now broke and their suicides was not uncommon

Buying on margin was an attempt to get rich quick; to get more than they were entitled to. It appears that THINGS were the most important part of their lives.

When a society abandons it's basic principles and moral values, the results are usually all bad and history shows us that the decade of the 1930's will bear this out.

CHAPTER 3

The Great Depression

We hear about Black Friday when referring to the stock market crash on October 29, 1929 but it was really a black Tuesday as the original term occurred on Friday September 24. 1869. It started because gold speculators were attempting to corner the gold market; since then, a plunging stock market has generally been referred to as Black Friday.

Friday or Tuesday makes little difference for on October 29, 1929 the market fell big time signaling the start of the great depression.

Times were so bad that unemployment hit 25%; that's one out of every four workers had no job. Compare that to the unemployment today in the United States and you can imagine how devastating this was to the country; by the way, the whole world was in the same boat.

If you ever have looked at pictures taken during the depression, you saw soup lines extending for city blocks to get a meal. That probably was the only meal that most of them would have that day

Men would dress and leave to go to work in the morning when they didn't have a job, because they were ashamed and embarrassed. In those days a man felt a strong responsibility to provide for his family. Unemployment benefits didn't start until 1936; so being unemployed meant, NO INCOME! I wonder if the men of today would feel the same way or would they just stay home and collect unemployment. Do you think they would feel it was the government's responsibility to take of them and their families?

Another factor so different from today is that very few wives worked outside the home so there was no falling back on the second income. Women really didn't start outside jobs until world war two when they needed to work because their men were off fighting the war. When the war ended and the men returned, the wives didn't want to return to the home. They had a taste of something different and for many, there was no going back

I saw on TV the riots taking place in Greece where the national debt was about to bankrupt the country. Greece is a true socialist country where the government provides everything for everyone; the only problem is there's never enough money so they borrow until they can't pay it back.

The European Union was willing to loan Greece a vast amount of money to resolve their debt but with the stipulation they cut spending. Spending cuts would require a reduction in the benefits the people now receive. The riots are because the people won't accept the cuts even though they are needed for the country to survive. Greece decided to let the people decide if they wanted to stay in the EU and cut spending to get the loan or go back to their old currency, the Drachma: by a close vote, the people decided to accept the cuts in benefits. Sometimes what appears to be generosity and caring, has selfish motives.

The EU is concerned that the problem in Greece will spread throughout Europe because there are many other countries in Europe in the same debt crisis as Greece. The United States is also sending money because we also worry that the crisis will spread to America; Of course we had to borrow the money since we don't bring in enough to pay our own operating expenses. Have you seen our debt lately? The United States is now one of the countries whose debt exceeds the total produced by our country in a year.

When things are really going bad, some people just tighten their belts and work extra hard to work their way out of their problems; however, work was really hard to find. The second choice was to hang out at the local beer garden and share horror stories with your friends who were in the same boat

My grandfather had a bar in the mid 30's named the Yellow Lantern. You could get a shupper of beer for 5 cents (a shupper was a Hugh mug).

You wouldn't think with money in such short supply, that beer would sell, but when it was time to open for business, they were already lined up around the corner. You have heard the saying about crying in your beer; this may have been where it originated.

Grandpa and Grandma lived in an apartment above the yellow lantern. One night just before Christmas he heard a noise downstairs and went to investigate. There were pinball machines in the bar and unlike the later machines, they paid money; you weren't allowed to put your hands on the machine, just shoot the ball and hope. When Grandpa arrived downstairs with his 20 gauge shotgun, there was a man perhaps in his 30's trying to get money from the machines; when he saw Grandpa with the shotgun, according to Grandpa, even in the poor light he could see his face turn ashen. He turned and ran through the front door without stopping to open it; the glass shattered and went everywhere.

Grandpa never fired his gun. He said times were so bad and it was Christmas; he figured maybe he was trying to get money to buy his kids Christmas.

Franklin Roosevelt is elected President in hopes of turning around the economy. Those that did have jobs were lucky to make $8.00 a week. My father told me you could buy a whole pig for $5.00, but no one had $5.00.

Roosevelt was elected by promising a New Deal, which was aimed at addressing the depression and high unemployment. The new deal included banking reform laws to prevent another depression, work relief programs and agriculture programs. Aid to tenant farmers and migrant workers came later along with Union protection programs and social security.

The New Deal programs helped in the near term. But in 1940, seven years after the start of these programs, the unemployment rate stood at 14.6 percent. The long term result was much worse as it allowed the Federal Government to get involved in the financial and personal affairs of the people. This has expanded over the years until there is very little about our lives that the government is not involved with either directly or indirectly. I do love old sayings; what's that one about "opening Pandora's box"?

My father started work for General Motors in Flint at the Fisher Body plant in 1928 where working conditions were pitiful. There were no breaks; they would come around with a bucket of water and a dipper that everyone drank from. They worked piece work, which means you were paid for the work produced not by the hour. Sometimes the line, which stretched for city blocks, would break down. Whatever time it took to repair it, you didn't get paid.

Workers had basically no rights and your foreman might come up to you and say he had to lay you off because a relative of his needed a job and they would reemploy you as soon as a position opens up.

They had telephones in the 1930's but GM refused to call if you were laid off. A worker had to be at the plant site about 5:00 AM to see if his name were called to return to work; anyone whose name was called and he was not there, lost his job. My father said there might be 500 workers outside the gate and they call back 15. In the winter it could be below zero while you show up day after day hoping to go back to work.

It was 1937 when the "Battle of Running Bulls" took place. This was the name given to the sit-down strike at General Motors Fisher Body Plant. The workers had formed a union in an attempt to get decent working conditions and a fair wage.

About 2000 workers occupied the plant and refused to leave so GM asks the police to physically remove them. Food and drink was brought in and in those days all bottles was glass. The empty bottles were stored in large wooden bins and when the police tried to enter the factory, there was a wall of bottles thrown; several police were carried out and according to my father, the police never tried that again.

The union had retained several tough characters to help them keep control of the plant. One day my father was looking out a second floor window when he saw a policeman fall on the ground; One of the hired toughs grabbed a piece of iron stock and threw it like a spear at the policeman; the rod went between his arm and chest, just inches from killing him. After several attempts by the police to evict the strikers failed, and violence was increasing, the Governor called in the National Guard. GM had hoped they would be used to evict the strikers but they were only there to keep the peace.

It's not that I'm totally pessimistic, but, having seen politics at work for so many years, could it possibly be that the Governor sat down with his pencil, and looking at the next election, calculated there were a lot more workers than executives at GM.

The Vice President of the United States favored evicting the workers but President Roosevelt did not, so after about six weeks of living in the Fisher Plant, my father went home. The union had an agreement that covered one page. It wasn't everything they hoped for, but it was a start.

The union presented a medallion to all the workers that went through the sit-down strike. One day last year I was watching Antiques Road Show when a man who had obtained the medallion, asks what it was. He was informed it was from the 1937 strike and had a value of about $850. I have my father's medallion along with his 25 year gold watch and a copy of the one page agreement. It's a bit ironic that he had to work about a year for that amount of money. I believe he told me they were averaging about 42 cents an hour when the strike began.

It was World War Two that really gave a boost to our economy. By 1943 the unemployment rate was below 2%. Financially we were in great shape but at a cost in lives of 406,000 men and women with another 671,000 injured.

With the financial catastrophe of the 1930's combined with the tremendous loss of lives in the first half of the 1940's; it's not at all surprising that America turned closer to God in their attitudes and how they lived their lives.

One interesting note is that right after the World Trade Centers collapsed from the Islamic Terrorist attack (yes I said Islamic) Bible sales skyrocketed. I wonder how many of those have ever been read or even opened. It's been thirteen years and humans are noted for very short memories, especially when it's convenient.

That's exactly what the Jews did under similar circumstances, maybe there's very little difference in how people interact with God no matter what their background; when life is good. It's God who; and when the bottom drops out it's; oh God I'm so sorry! Can you help?

Chapter 4

Lifestyles in the 40's and 50's

When I look back over my life from my birth in 1939 to present day 2018 I have witnessed unbelievable changes both good and bad.

The good has raised our standard of living, provided great advancements in medical, dental and communications just to mention a few.

The typical home in the 1940's was less than half the size of today's homes. The lots were very small because of cost but also upkeep. There were only push mowers as power mowers were not available yet. Most people living today have never used a push mower and if you have, you know what a job it was to cut your yard. Life sometimes does tend to repeat itself.

Many young couples now are buying homes with yards as small, not because they don't have the money and power mowers make the job much easier; they don't want the upkeep and are willing to sacrifice the privacy. It's not uncommon to see subdivisions with homes in the $300,000 to $600,000 range with literally no front or back yard and 10 feet between houses. We have become such a busy society that we no longer have time to enjoy the simple things in life like landscaping the yard, planting a garden or putting up a bad minten net for family fun.

Automobiles in the early 50's didn't come with a heater or radio as these were options. The engines would have to be rebuilt after 50,000 miles. Today, the typical auto has two to three times the horsepower, every option known to man, and engines that get 200,000 to 300,000 miles. Not every family had an auto and two car families were limited to the higher income, while today we have families with three, four and more. Only a very few students in high school had cars and they were very old so you didn't need land for parking spaces Our high school parking lots today are larger than the entire school property in the 50's.

Calculators came on the scene for every day use soon to be replaced by the computer I started to work for IBM in 1965. The model 360 which many experts thought only a handful of the largest companies in the world would be potential customers, were selling like hotcakes. Today the cheapest smallest home computer has more memory and far greater speed than multi million dollar computers at corporate giants.

Very few Americans had ever flown on an airplane let alone ever traveled out of the country. The only view of the world for most came from magazines, movies or TV. Now, the skies are filled with commercial aircraft. Teens have been to Europe, even if their parents have not.

Speaking of TV; in the 50's they were black & white with screens about the size of the computer screen today. There were only a few channels and they went off the air at midnight playing the National Anthem. The quality was poor and that is being very generous. Many homes had a TV antennae on their roof or on a tower next to the house; even then the picture would often lose sync and either roll vertically or pull horizontally. Today we enjoy over 200 channels that never go off the air, in color, on screens of 40, 50 and 60 inches.

Eating out was a rare commodity. There were very few restaurants and most were family owned. All of the chains that we are familiar with today did not exist. The first fast food restaurant in Flint was a McDonalds that opened about 1954. Hamburgers were 10 cents and cheeseburgers were 12 cents. No, all the options you find at today's McDonalds were not available.

My Grandparents had a cottage on a small lake about 120 miles north of Flint. On the drive to the cottage we had about three places to stop and eat. This should give you some idea of how seldom people ate out. Today, look at your yellow pages and count the restaurants.

Americans today enjoy medical and dental care that was only dreamed of in the 1950's. Ulcerated Colitis is still a serious illness but unlike my mother who had to die at the age of 36 leaving four children a person today can live! A major secret to a long life is early detection and the tests that are available now make that possible.

Drugs that are available today didn't exist; therefore, people suffered and died. Before penicillin was discovered, when a person contacted pneumonia they went through a crisis period that determined if they lived or died.

Dental practices mimicked the medical profession. In the 1950's when your face swelled up which meant you had an abysses tooth, you went to the dentist and had it pulled. If you only had a tooth ache, it was filled. There was no such thing as a root canal or implants. No one had their teeth cleaned so if you developed gum disease, they pulled all your teeth and you got dentures.

Just from the few things I mentioned, you can see how advances in medical and dental have increased the quality and length of our lives; while technology has increased productivity and along with it came previously unknown prosperity. Two income families also helped make it possible for families to have more THINGS!

In 1947, two years after the war ended, only 28 percent of the women were in the workforce. In 2000 64 percent of women between 24 and 54 years of age were in the workforce.

Single income families and no welfare programs sometimes required a part time job to supplement your income when an emergency arose and family members were also there to help out; now our society depends on the Government for assistance, which in reality of course, is our friends and neighbors since that is where the Government gets its money.

Welfare and other assistance programs have done far more harm to our society than it has good; not only has it taken the responsibility away from the people to care for themselves and their family members, but has created an attitude that a good life is owed to them by others in society.

I want to continue to stress the fact that the Government only establishes bad programs; the people pay for them and in so doing lower the standard of living for their own family.

I have discovered that almost nothing in life is ever all good or all bad, and this good life financially, has resulted in devastating changes to the American culture. More about this later.

CHAPTER 5

The Start of Decline (the 1960's)

Actually it is my belief that the decline in a very small way started in 1956 when Elvis Presley appeared on the Ed Sullivan show. Ed Sullivan had previously stated that he would never have Elvis on his show because his lower body gyrations were sensual and provocative and unsuitable for television. After Elvis appeared on the Steve Allen Show which had twice the viewers that night as Ed Sullivan, he changed his mind and signed him for three shows.

When you look at today's world this must seem like a no brainer but it does let us know one important fact; money and success will turn a person's head and help them to accept what they previously didn't believe in. What Ed Sullivan thought was not proper for TV viewing became ok if his show gained viewing audience.

The real problem is not so much the gyrations of Elvis as acceptance by those that felt it was not proper. Ed Sullivan was motivated by money and success; while others wanted to fit in and Elvis was such a hit their feelings would not be well received. The parents had children that idolized Elvis and they wouldn't want their children to be mad at them because it was more important to be their friends than their parents.

Elvis was a little ole country boy from Tupelo Mississippi and I think the entertainment world was a bit more that he could comfortably handle. He was often referred to as the king, but his response was "there is only one King" He was of course referring to Jesus for he had been raised in the church and counted himself a Christian.

Have you ever noticed that change, either good or bad, starts ever so gradual so that it's hardly even noticed and if it is, most people just say, that's such a small thing it's not worth worrying about

The exception to the ever so gradual statement is the Obama administration and the democrat congress. It appears they wanted to change everything in America in one fell swoop and the people are angry and concerned. You would think they would have learned not to bite off more than you can chew.

On the other hand, maybe they decided that the average American today is so involved in obtaining "the good life", that the most they will do is complain. We have seen the Tea Party groups taking a strong stand, but there should be tens of millions protesting, calling, and writing their Senators and Congressmen.

The real significant change started small in San Francisco and eventually spread across America; the Hippie movement. The Hippie movement infiltrated Canada and Europe as well but not like the United States.

Hippies came from all walks of life but more from the wealthy middle class families. Their families were conservative, religious people, their children, many of them obviously spoiled, they rebelled and rejected their parent's values. They didn't go to church or work unless they absolutely had to. They used LSD and Marijuana and practiced free love. They were generally rejected by adult society as a whole but I believe they had a huge impact on the youth. The youth of the sixties are the baby boomers of today.

Many of the former Hippies would tell you today that they were against the Vietnam War and against racism which was all well and good, but how did that justify being lazy, dirty, immoral, and illegal drug users. There were plenty of everyday people that also were against those things but didn't live like Hippies. It is amazing how we are able to come up with justification for bad behavior.

The Hippie movement was the real beginning in America of rebellion against society's values and rules; actually, most of society's standards and how we are to live are based on the Bible, at least they used to be. It's interesting that in the Bible; one of God's prophets complaining to God how that the people rejected his word was informed by God" it's not you they are rejecting, it's me". When you think about it, if we didn't use the Bible to establish our laws and lifestyles, what would we use? If we allowed our leaders to determine the values and morals for our country wouldn't it change with each change of leadership? We have the courts to keep things in check, don't we? This is another subject for later discussion.

My father told all of his children when they were teenagers; the day you decide to leave home and go on your own you assume the role of an adult who takes responsibility for your life. He wanted his children to be accountable for their actions and their decisions.

I totally agree with my father's position and feel it is irresponsible on the part of parents that bail their grown children out of situations of their own doing. I read some time ago in a magazine article about grown children moving back home, that the father was somewhat distraught that his thirty five year old son had moved home because he was having difficulty making payments on his Corvette and luxury apartment. Gee, I guess it would be cruel of dad to say, no son, sell the Corvette and buy a sub compact and move to a less expensive apartment and then one day if you can afford that lifestyle, you can upscale. Of course that would be holding the child accountable for his/her own life and expecting them to make sacrifices instead of the parents.

During one of my trips to my home state of Michigan I was setting on the front porch talking with my father when he brought up the subject of the union. He was disappointed and disgusted with what they had become. This was the man that lived in the shop for six weeks to form that union. He said as bad as working conditions were before and the greed of executives, the union was even worse. They made demands that were unreasonable and selfish.

I ask him why when he attended the union meeting didn't he stand up and tell them what they were demanding was not the purpose of the 1937 strike. They were looking for fair pay and working conditions and now the union's demands were ridiculous. He said, son, you don't understand, the union has some tough guys that oversee the meeting and if I objected to their plans, after I was yelled down by my fellow workers, you would find me in the alley with both my arms broken. I might also find the tires on my car slashed by my fellow workers when I was ready to leave work. My father really was an idealist; he thought the people he worked with would be different than the executives at GM, but he was wrong. Power indeed does corrupt and it doesn't make any difference if you're a high paid executive, or a blue collar worker.

Car pooling was common in those days and my father and four of his friends from work would each drive for a week. This not only saved money but left the car home four out of five weeks for the wife; remember there weren't many two car families. The same guys bowled on a team once a week for many years.

My father's friends kept asking him to run for committeeman which was a union representative. If a union member had a complaint he went to his committeeman for resolution. He told them he didn't want the job but they kept asking him so one day he solved the problem. He told me the last time they ask me to take the job I replied; if the shop foreman (who was non union management) was to come to me and informed me one of the workers had come to work drunk and wanted to fire him; I would say, go ahead; You know they never ask me to be their committeeman again.

What normally happened in this situation was the committeeman would tell the foreman, if you try to fire my man we will shut down the line in protest. This could cost the company millions in lost production. The worker was not fired and he helped build the car you purchased. Is it surprising the quality of cars in those days was so bad? The work ethic and basic values are starting to change and with it the lack of accountability is starting to grow.

If you look at Consumer Reports Magazine over the years you see that the Japanese cars always beat out the American cars and values and work ethic made the difference. On the American assembly line when a car reaches the end of the line and has problems, they divert it to the repair line. The problems are the result of poor quality workmanship. The Japanese operate differently; if a car has a problem, the line is shut down until it is resolved and the person responsible feels shame in front of his fellow workers. Now this is accountability. Recently the Japanese auto makers have experienced quality problems mostly in the design area. Could it be they are becoming too westernized?

American autos have gradually improved in quality from the 60's and 70's but mainly because of the competition from the Japanese not by a change in attitude of the American worker.

I had a 1970 Buick Electra, top of the Buick line that the paint on the hood developed thousands of tiny cracks which we found was due to no primer being applied before it was painted. How does this even happen on an assembly line? My aunt had told me when she worked assembling transmissions that some of the workers would flip their cigarette butts into the transmissions before sealing them up.

It's 1965 and IBM was hiring because the IBM 360 computer was shipping and they needed people due to the volume of orders. While values and work ethic were starting to change, it wasn't so at IBM. This was the premier company in the US. Tomas Watson Jr. was the CEO. His father Thomas Watson Sr. had moved the company from butcher scales to tabulators and typewriters.

It was reported that Watson Jr. gambled the future of IBM on the development of the 360 computers; this was in spite of the fact most experts didn't think there was much of a market for the 360 computers; maybe a handful of the largest companies would be interested; they were wrong. In 1965 the gross revenue was 3.75 billion and in 2008 103 billion.

The five years until 1970 working for IBM was fantastic. Orders for the 360 computers were coming in faster than we could fill them; talk about busy, and the pressure was intense but with it came rewards. IBM under Watson was an employee and family oriented business if you could excel the company recognized it and were generous in giving rewards. Up to this time the changing work ethic and rebellious attitudes had not affected IBM, but change was in the air.

Chapter 6

American values are changing fast (1970's and beyond)

It's about 1971 or 72 and all the managers from the Memphis office are attending the yearly area managers meeting in New Orleans. The area covered several southern states. This particular meeting was quite different from previous ones. A professor from Berkeley in California was the keynote speaker. He looked like a 60's hippie with hair down to his waist and a beard to match. Keep in mind, IBM still required white shirts and suit and tie. Hair and beard like the professor's would never be accepted.

The reason IBM brought in such a non typical speaker was to prepare the managers for the new age employee. The professor proceeded to describe the difference in the employees they would be hiring and the employees that currently work for IBM. One of the differences will be that they would not have company loyalty; He went on to describe various traits that IBM managers had never had to deal with; most of them not well accepted. One of our managers became so disgusted he left the meeting; whereas the area manager instructed him to return to the meeting.

IBM has always been a company that sees the handwriting on the wall and gets a head start dealing with it; the one exception was their delay in entering the personal computer market; as a result they never did really compete. They were waiting to see how they went over. This wasn't the Thomas Watson approach; he had foresight and took risk. I believe sometimes when a company takes risk and is successful, they have a tendency to get conservative and protect what they have achieved. This may have been the case with the personal computer.

But IBM did recognize the change coming with people and the old values and principles of the past were about to die and IBM would have to change with it whether they liked it or not. Almost no one ever quit IBM and that was also about to change. The professor explained the new generation employee might work 5 years and move to another company or even change professions. Don't expect them to stay with the company and retire from there. The seven hours of testing required in 1965, went by the wayside; I don't know if they felt the new generation couldn't pass them or it was part of the affirmative action program; I suspect it was the latter. Affirmative action means the company lowers the hiring standards so some minorities can obtain higher paying jobs that they are not qualified for.

The government was putting pressure on companies that it purchased their products or services to hire minorities and most companies bent to the pressure. Money talks, so instead of saying we will make every effort to find qualified minorities but we will not lower our standards; if they couldn't find enough qualified people, they hired marginal performers.

The IBM area management sent a black graduate engineer from a black college to the Memphis office to be interviewed and hired. The manager assigned to interview him was a top manager who had won manager of the year awards. He tested the man on electronics (remember he was a graduate electrical engineer) and he failed the test miserably. The manager trying to give him every break thought maybe he just choked up taking written tests so he gave him an oral test. His oral test was even worse; the man didn't even know how to measure a diode in a circuit. Basic electronics school students would know how.

When the manager informed the area office that he could not hire the man because he wasn't qualified, they accused him of being a racist. Fortunately, the branch manager in Memphis was a tough cookie and a fair man who supported his manager. This episode shows how badly IBM wanted to meet their quota of minorities; they were willing to accept a non qualified man.

Affirmative action totally contradicts the concept in America that you get what you earn, but is a socialist program designed to reward people above their level of expertise or competence. You can't make everyone equal no mater how you try. Anyone who has children knows you may have one that's a doctor and one that teaches first grade. They have different abilities, and different interests. Their lifestyles will never be equal unless you take part of the doctors income and give it to the teacher; income redistribution. I can't imagine any reasonable parent being supportive of such a plan; so why do we let our government attempt redistribution of wealth?

When you look at IBM today they have done away with the retirement plan and offer 401K plans instead. Many of the benefits that every IBM employee enjoyed in the 60's and 70's have one by one been terminated. The same is true for most companies. As the employees attitudes and values changed so did the companies. Maybe that not so old saying (what goes around, comes around) could apply here.

In the late 60's early 70's the schools are starting to change, but keep in mind, schools don't change, people do. We often make statements like the world is really changing when we should be saying; the people in the world are really changing. Inanimate objects are not capable of changing, only people.

The changes then were tiny when compared with what is happening in our schools today. Remember what I said previously; change almost always starts so small that everyone ignores it, and ignores it again, and again, until they're shocked at where it has arrived, and then it's so imbedded it's almost impossible to correct

We can already see the results of decline in education by the early 70's. In 1973 the Navy and Army found it necessary to rewrite many of their manuals to a ninth grade level because so many of their high school graduates read at that level. This should have been a wake up call for educators and especially for parents. Parents should not have counted on the education system to ensure their children received a proper education, but they obviously didn't get involved because the SAT scores continued to drop each year and when American students are compared to students in other countries, they do poorly.

A company in the United States when offered the so called stimulus package funds by the Obama administration which were supposed to reduce unemployment, wanted to hire all employees from other countries; the reason being I'm sure, they are better qualified and have a better work ethic.

For those who watched the debates between Obama and McCain; in one of them the question was ask of McCain; since our students perform near the bottom when compared to other countries in the free world, what would you do to improve education? Part of McCain's response pointed out that we spend more money per student and our students spend more hours in school. One could reasonably conclude that the statistics show that neither money nor hours in the classroom have done anything to improve our student's achievement. Why then would Obama respond when ask the same question; we need to spend more money and more days in school? I believe both politicians realized the answer lies with the students and their parents. There is really nothing the government can do to reverse this downward trend.

I don't mean to let the school system off the hook, they certainly played a part in the decline, but for the most part today, their hands are tied. The education system is so hamstrung by the parents, courts and school leaders which include principles and school board members; they can't do the job they were hired to do.

If teachers fail students that don't perform at grade level it reflects on their teaching ability, and in some cases it should, but in others, the students just haven't applied themselves; the results; pass them on through. One of the problems is so many would have to be held back there are not enough schools to handle it; what ever happened to full time summer school? The answer is, the parents. My daughter who is a teacher said the school can't afford summer school and my response was; make the parents pay!

There was a case in California several years ago where a man sued the school system because they graduated him and when he applied for a job discovered he couldn't read. How does a student attend school for twelve years unable to read? Why didn't some teacher discover the fact? No accountability! By the way, he lost the case!

Compare how the school system operated in the 1950's with today. In grammar school each student was required to stand up and read one paragraph from a story. You didn't know in advance what story the teacher might select so you better know how to read. If they still did that today, no student would escape detection concerning their reading ability. Early detection, like in healthcare, results in a cure.

Homework has all but been eliminated in most schools: supposedly doing homework doesn't help that much; whatever happened to "practice makes perfect"? The teachers and parents appear to have gone along with this idea. Could it possibly be because teachers no longer have to grade homework papers and the parents don't have to ensure their child does the homework?

Perhaps it would profit their child more to spend the time playing video games and the child will be much happier; and for the parents and teachers; no confrontation. Just think of the great job opportunities for a first class game player; not to mention the contribution they will make to society.

How about student accountability for their conduct? I explained how it was when I went to school; teachers punished you in a variety of ways and this didn't end with grade school. I can remember in Junior high which went through the 9th grade, being paddled at the front of the class with a wooden paddle made by the woodshop instructor. He would drill holes in the paddle so the air wouldn't slow it down. I'm not sure which end of my anatomy was redder, my behind or my face. We don't have corporal punishment in today's schools as the parents would not allow it. Why would the parents allow punishment at school when they don't punish them at home? The students now know they won't be held accountable for their actions and it shows in their conduct and attitude. The parents are the main ones responsible and their not held accountable either.

Discipline no longer exists in our public schools and many good teachers have left the profession as a result. The last opportunity to keep our schools a decent place to teach and to learn rested on the shoulders of the court system and sadly, they have played a major role in the decline of public education. The courts have become so engrossed with individual rights (the me, myself, and I syndrome) that the welfare of society as a whole gets trampled on. Students can use profanity, even against teachers under the protection of the courts interpretation of freedom of speech. They also get involved in what restrictions can be placed on the students: all of this fueled by the parents.

Curving of grades is a classic example of a lack of accountability. If you're not familiar with grade curving, it works like this; if the highest grade received by the students on a test was an 80; then 80 will be an "A" and we work down from there. At this point we don't know if the teacher did a poor job of teaching the material, or the students didn't apply themselves; but whichever the case, someone is not being held accountable. The parents think their student is doing well based on the bogus mark, but the reality is, the student's education suffers. It was recently reported that some schools are considering doing away with grades altogether, another great decision to make our students less able to compete with students from other countries.

Parents keep their children out of school for everything from trips to Disney World to beach vacations, and who is held accountable?; no one!

The sad part isn't as much the parents that support their children's rebellious attitudes and disrespectful conduct, as the parents who have allowed such degradation of the public school system because they don't want confrontation.

Their children don't want their parents to rock the boat because they might be harassed or not accepted by their peers.

When we avoid controversy which almost always results in confrontation, things go terribly wrong, or if already wrong, most likely get worse and never get fixed.

When homework, discipline and expectation of proper conduct were no longer a requirement by parents and teachers, coupled with grades given that had not been earned, we ended up with the pitiful results we see today.

Why then do we think that the person we put in office, whether it is at the local, state or federal level could do anything to turn education around? You have to have laws and rules for society that government is responsible to enforce, but these are for the handful of rebellious and irresponsible souls. For a society to function properly the majority must be responsible, moral, honest, and reliable; when that is no longer the case, the rules are almost impossible to enforce.

We had four daughters in Oakhaven School in Memphis which was a neighborhood school that covered kindergarten through twelve grades. This was the generation that the educational system decided to experiment with by introducing Modern Math. You would have thought the educators by now would have figured out that not everyone will be proficient in every subject. Modern math was supposed to make sure that a student understood math not just memorizes the procedure to arrive at the correct answer.

I happen to like math and have always done well with the subject; but if there is a single subject that in my opinion the fewest people like or understand, it would be math. If it wasn't so serious I would have rolled on the floor when I saw what they were doing. If the problem was multiplying 6x5, it required a whole page of steps to arrive at the answer 30. I felt from the beginning this experiment was going to be a failure and the students wouldn't know how to use the old methods that had been in use for decades. I decided to teach my children the old method parallel with the school's method.

Well it turned out to be an abject failure and a whole generation of students was less capable in math than before. I would have thought that wise educators (and I'm not implying that all educators are wise) would have tried a pilot program with a few students that were not proficient in math to verify if the program worked before implementing it for the entire system.

Another change was taking place when the Latin teacher gave the students an assignment to attend an "R" rated movie for class work and it was required. I informed the teacher that my daughters were not allowed to attend "R" rated movies and that she would have to provide an alternate work, which she did. What showed me how people's values and principles were changing was not so much the teacher who gave such an assignment, but the fact that I was the only parent in her entire class that objected and did not allow their child to attend.

Martin Luther King had been assassinated in Memphis in 1968 and discrimination was the topic of the day. Why does it seem like whenever someone tries to correct a problem they almost always go overboard and make decisions that defy logic?

A low income housing development was about to open and all the children would be attending Oakhaven school. The principle had a PHD which means he was educated but not necessarily had any common sense.

If I may digress for a moment to make this statement; our early presidents had little or no experience and certainly not the education available today but were able to make great decisions because they had common sense and the ability to reason successfully.

Back to subject at hand; the principle rather than wait until the end of the semester decided to integrate the children from the low income housing into all the classes which would require that students that had already received their first six weeks mark be transferred to other classes with different teachers.

It that wasn't bad enough, one of my daughters who was in advanced classes, would be transferred to regular classes so students from the low income could attend advanced classes and that was without determining if they would even qualify.

The straw that broke the principle's back, was when I found out the school couldn't work out a schedule for her history, so after receiving a mark in history, they were to transfer her to a science class and her history mark would count as the first grade in science.

To say this was unacceptable, dishonest, and probably illegal is an understatement. I arranged a conference with the principle to discuss the situation. I explained that the only logical solution was to wait until the end of the semester; whereas he informed me that since most of the children from the low income housing were black, he could receive flack for not integrating them into all the classes right away.

I proceeded to request that he handle the flack since it was totally unreasonable to transfer students to different teachers in the middle of the semester because he was afraid of being accused of racism. When he told me he had already made up his mind, I informed him he left me no choice but to take the issue to the school board. His response was "you can take it to the Board but in the end it will be done my way" Do we detect a bit of arrogance?

What really amazes me is that people want to avoid controversy and fit in and be accepted by their peers so bad, that they will even turn against those that are trying to help them. Once my daughters friends who were also being forced to transfer, found out her father was going to the school board, they turned on her and said I was wrong to do that.

The School Board agreed to give me five minutes during their meeting to state my case. The school principle was required to attend if it was necessary to dispute any of my claims.

I presented the principle's plan to the board emphasizing removing students from advanced classes and my big gun; giving credit for attending a science class when it was really history because that was the only way he could make his plan work. The board couldn't believe he was willing to falsify school records. The board members ask if I had talked to the principle before taking the issue to the School Board.

Military training is helpful in many ways and one of those is the rule; never go over the head of the person in charge without giving them the opportunity to resolve the problem first

I told them I had and when he refused to resolve the issue I had informed him of my intention to go to the board. Now I believe that the facts were ample to prove my case and the results probably would have been the same, but a little frosting on the cake never hurts, so I explained that the principle's response was basically, in the end it will be done my way. The principal was saying he already knew how the board would rule; oh, don't we hate to be taken for granted.

Maybe it was the last statement but even I was taken back by the way the board chewed out the principle and instructed him to change his plan and restore things to normal.

The next day the principle met with me and my daughter and most likely was instructed to do so by the board. He wasn't the arrogant man of our previous meeting but came with hat in hand and assured me that everything would be corrected immediately.

Now all of my daughters friends who were mad at her, now loved her dearly which goes to prove that most people will criticize, insult and provide no support when your battling a controversial subject, but once you win they want to wallow in the victory. Now it's true that these were children, but I find that as adults we're even worse. We still hate the conflict because we have seen the problems connected with it, but now we are so busy with what's important to us, we refuse to get involved no matter how important the issue.

It is my belief that in general, our society in America today for the most part has only three people that are important in their lives; me, myself and I. There have been many references to the "me generation" so I'm just providing them with a couple more people to love that they will accept.

I think it's safe to say that the school system is changing and not for the better. Could it be because the people are becoming more rebellious, arrogant and generally unconcerned with their fellow man no matter what the results of their decisions might be?

The education system has been a major contributor to influencing young people to change the way they think, and how you think reflects in how you live. We know today that the majority of people in the teaching profession tend to be quite liberal and they have the perfect forum to indoctrinate their students, and what makes it perfect is they know the parents are so involved in their own lives they won't take the time to monitor what's happening in their child's school. Oh, there may be a few parents who may complain but with little or no support nothing will be done.

In 1973 we transferred to Raleigh North Carolina and the daughter that I managed to keep in her classes in Memphis attended Millbrook Junior high which I believe is now a grade school.

One of her classes was North Carolina history and American Heritage. Now you wouldn't think you would have to battle the school in class like this, but the title was deceiving. There were two teachers; A man and wife team that were allowed to write the curriculum for the class. I made it a practice to always review everything that was being used to teach my children for I knew change was in the air and the school system could not be trusted.

In the workbook developed by these teachers, statements like you can't accept everything your parents teach you because a lot of it is just tradition. There were other statements that demeaned the United States; demeaning the United States is not uncommon today but it was just beginning in 1973; remember my saying change seldom happens all at once but starts small and when no one objects begins to grow, what did this have to do with North Carolina History? The school principle did not want to provide me with a copy of the guide but after I ask if he would rather have me check with the school board, he rethought his position.

After reviewing the guide I made copies of the controversial statements that I felt would certainly offend most parents and provided them to my neighborhood, after which I called a meeting at my house to develop a plan of action to resolve the problem. There were about 240 homes in our neighborhood and only one woman showed up! I guess they were just too busy making money and living the good life to be bothered with what their children were being taught.

I went to the principle and had my daughter transferred to another class. I handled my responsibility but was disappointed that I was unable to put a stop to such indoctrination; this was a case of liberal educators wanting to change the way there students believed especially if their parents had taught them conservative values.

About year or two later, a group of neighbors showed up at my door wanting to talk to me about running for a county commissioner; it seems they were concerned about the direction the school system was taking and thought I would be the man to gets things back on the right track. These were the same parents that didn't show up for the meeting. I thanked them for considering me for the position, but told them I felt they were a bit late; many changes have been implemented since that meeting and were pretty much set in concrete. I respectfully rejected their idea and suggested they find someone else for the job. After they left I thought what they are trying to do now is close the barn door after the horse has run away. I can't help quoting these sayings because they seem to apply to so many situations we encounter in life.

My neighbors were correct to be worried about what was happening to the public education system but we need to quit talking about systems and other things; it's always about changes in people. What was happening to education were the changing values and principles of people; when you couple this with the fact that many parents are selfish and mainly interested in their own lives, change became so easy to implement and most of it bad.

Articles were coming out stating that Johnny can't read which was pointing out how poorly our students was performing in school. The SAT scores were declining every year and there were obvious reasons, still no one took any action to fix the problems.

The conservative members of congress, both state and federal governments, have been trying for years to establish a voucher system, which I strongly approve of. This system would give parents a voucher in the amount spent per child on public education so they would be able to choose the school they wanted their children to attend. Some may decide to keep them in public schools and others in charter or private schools.

The reason most parents have to leave their children in the public system is because they can't afford to be taxed for public education and pay for private schools out of their own pocket; which results in their paying twice for education.

Now the public teachers union is opposed to this for obvious reasons; there would be less need for public school teachers; although jobs would open up in the private sector. Since we already know the majority of teachers and professors are liberal; they wouldn't enjoy the freedom to indoctrinate their students in a private school environment like they can in the public schools.

Keep in mind that the students in private schools outperform those in the public sector; therefore, the teachers union in more interested in their own agenda, than the welfare of their students.

They claim vouchers would mean the end of public education, which I seriously doubt. I believe the very liberal parents would keep their children in the public schools because social agenda and indoctrination are more important to them than reading, writing and arithmetic.

Doesn't it literally blow your mind that so many of the politicians that oppose vouchers have their children enrolled in private schools? They have money and can afford to do what they know you will be unable to do without a voucher system. Maybe they just don't want their children to have to hobnob with the lower class. They must think the private school is better; otherwise, why pay tuition for what is available for free?

It is my belief that the politicians want to keep your children in public schools as part of their interest in social engineering. They will reprogram your children to think in a more progressive (liberal) manner. If you don't see that happening in your schools today; you need to apply for a government grant for the visually impaired.

It would be refreshing to be able to end the discussion on the sorry state of our public school system on a positive note. In Wake County, North Carolina, the people elected 5 new School Board members that ran on a pledge to return to neighborhood schools' all five were elected and now make up the majority.

The Superintendent under the previous liberal School Board had implemented bussing for the purpose of diversity. Now that the new board was going to do away with his diversity program, he decided to resign, which the new board gladly accepted.

This infuriated the far left and the NAACP which protested at the board meetings; however, the new board members stood by their pledge to those that elected them and bussing for diversity is over.

The fact that the School Board would implement such a program for the purpose of diversity shows that educators are more interested in social engineering than basic education. The cost of bussing, the time spent traveling, and separation from other children in their area should never have been approved. Where were the parents? I was pleased that they came to their senses enough to go to the polls and vote for conservative change. Since that change, most of the conservative members have left as the parents are becoming more liberal so what appeared to be a possible return to neighborhood schools and some common sense applied to our education system was just a fleeting hope.

The NAACP threatened to sue, but the Supreme Court several years ago, decided that bussing is no longer required. Maybe there is still hope of turning around our education system; at least this was a step in the right direction. It now appears conservatism is losing out and the honeymoon is over and were back to the old ways.

One of the most divisive issues in America came from a Supreme Court decision in 1973; Roe VS Wade; a woman's right to have an abortion. Abortion was always illegal from the days of the founding fathers but that was now being challenged. This issue has divided the country as no other and I feel it was the catalyst to remove biblical principles from the running of our country and future decisions affecting all walks of life.

When the writings of our forefathers are reviewed, it becomes apparent that they were basing their beliefs on Judeo-Christian concepts; the old and new testaments. When they wrote about separation of Church and State, they were referring to their desire to keep the government from imposing any state religion on the people, or interfering in the practice of their religion, providing of course their religion didn't violate the law.

There was no way that practicing Christians could ever believe that Jesus would ever condone aborting your child for birth control. Having to choose between the mother and child or in the case of rape or incest is another matter, but most abortions are not for these cases but for birth control. There are no actual figures available but most studies place them at 1 percent or less of total abortions; when I say practicing Christians, I mean Born Again Christians; more about that later. Since less than 1% are for rape or incest, the other 99% must be for birth control and the majority are for women that are not married and don't want a child, so how come the pro-choice people refer to the right to abortion as a woman's health issue?

The other concern for Christians is what the response would be from God. I pointed out previously that when God withholds his blessings, things start to go downhill rapidly and he was not going to be happy with the court's decision. If this happened, the entire country could be negatively affected.

I believe the Court ignored the moral (Godly) issue of abortion and made their decision based on their concept of individual rights as they interpreted it to mean in the constitution. No reasonable person can possibly think that the founding fathers would have believed that their writing concerning individual rights would ever be interpreted to endorse abortion.

Supreme Court Justices with all their experience are still just humans and throughout the decades many of their decisions reflect their own views, rather than the intent of the framers of the constitution.

A recent statement by Justice Stevens, one of the most liberal Supreme Court justices in which he stated words to the effect; the constitution should be interpreted to fit modern living. If the Justices do that, they will in effect be changing the constitution without the required vote of the states.

Most Americans think the greatest power lies with the president or the congress, but they are wrong; both houses of congress can approve a law or a change in an existing law and the president can sign it; but if the law is challenged as unconstitutional, the Supreme Court can strike down the law, and they can use their own view of the meaning of the constitution to do it; now who has the most power?

The issue of whether forcing people to purchase health insurance Is constitutional, went before the courts, and ended up at the Supreme Court. About twenty one states challenged the Obama administration health care bill that was approved by congress. The court decide the government does have a right under the constitution to force a person to purchase health care insurance, but it is a tax even though the President insists it is not a new tax. I have always believed the Government could require a person to purchase health insurance as long as they called it by its proper name, a tax. Don't all working Americans have to pay a payroll tax to purchase health insurance for when they reach the age of 65? Medicare is going broke and Obama care will be an even greater disaster.

In today's rebellious America, you hear frequently of activist judges that no longer follow the law as written, but take it upon themselves to rule the way they think. This is becoming an increasingly frequent occurrence; expect it to get worse.

CHAPTER 7

America converting to Socialism?

Someone sent an article to me where the author discussed why a Democracy only survives about two hundred years. Since the leaders are elected by the people, it reaches a point where their only hope of getting elected is by promising free things and services to the people (I guess you could call that, buying the vote). Eventually, there isn't enough money or resources to provide what the people demand and we end up with a dictator who makes all the decisions without input from the people.

I suspect in the conversion from a democracy to a dictator, we are bound to pass through a socialist system; after all socialism is about providing for people by spreading the wealth even though there's never enough to go around.

Chavez in Venezuela, while listed as a socialist, had taken control of business including oil, shut down newspapers, TV stations and radio stations that he didn't agree with. He had to fix prices on food due to run away inflation and they live with brown outs due to power shortages.

To me, the most intriguing thing about Venezuela is that the people elected a man by a large majority that would take away their rights mainly because he would take away from those better off and give it to them. Redistribution of wealth is popular in a country with a large population of poor; however this philosophy has never proven to be successful. When a person's incentive to improve their life is hampered or removed, they lose their will to excel and fail to produce at whatever job they do; the result is a drop in quantity and quality; the standard of living of the whole of society goes down the drink.

At this time the citizens of Venezuela are leaving in droves to adjoining countries to find food and medicine which are not available in Venezuela; over 100,000 just to Columbia alone. The average wage is about $16.00 a day.

I use Venezuela as an example because I believe our country is headed in the same direction; at least if the democrats and their far left supporters have their way. This will only be possible if the American people set on their laurels and do nothing to stop it.

The latest poll shows about 33% of college kids approve of socialism. They have been brain washed by their liberal professors into believing this is the best system and that they will be given everything for free; I wonder how they would like living on $ 16.00 a day.

During the great depression a Democrat, Franklin Roosevelt in an effort to turn around the economy, implemented several socialist programs and it's been down hill ever since.

One of the programs Roosevelt implemented was Social Security and the main purpose was to keep the elderly out of poverty; in the depression about 50% of the elderly were poverty stricken. It was a mandatory program as it is today but did not cover all Americans.

The original rate was 1% on the first $3000 income for both the employee and the employer, which converts to $30 per year for each. The rate was to increase over the years to 3% on $3000 per year income and at the top rate would be paying $90 a year in Social Security deductions. I think you would be surprised to discover how many Americans are not even aware that their employer has to pay the same amount as they do; when they see how much was taken out of their paycheck each year they need to think double.

The employer has to count the Social Security payment as part of your benefit package and if he didn't have to pay it, he could pay the money to you; the result is you pay twice as much as you see on your year end earnings statement.

The maximum a person could pay in Social Security taxes in 2010 is $ 6621, add your employer's share and you were paying a maximum of $13,242; remember the top rate was projected to be $180 a year. We've come a long way baby. (Did you like that Virginia Slims ad)?

When Social Security is mentioned we automatically think of retirement benefits, but the plan is involved in much more. The plan is a social welfare and insurance system which covers disability, survivorship and death plus Medicare and Medicaid; How about unemployment benefits, temporary assistance to needy families, and my favorite Supplemental Security Income. Many of the benefits people were expected to take care of themselves, usually by purchasing life insurance, but now we have big brother involved and the cost is unbelievable.

Supplemental Security Income can be paid to immigrants when they reach age 65 that have never paid one cent into Social Security.

The Social Security program has been amended so many times by different administrations that it would require an entire book to list them and their impact, so I am only going to cover a few.

Benefits were not to be taxed in the original plan but by the 1980's the plan was in financial trouble so congress made 50% of your social security taxable if you as a couple made more than $32,000 a year. It wasn't long before the congress raised that to 85%.

Let's say you're a person who didn't just count on social security for your income and invested in an IRA or 401k plan. You reach 70 1/2 years of age and you must start withdrawing a set amount of money. You now discover that the additional income moves you into the 85% taxable bracket. You now pay taxes on the IRA or 401K distribution, but also pay more tax on your social security. Keep in mind those making less than $32,000 a year don't pay taxes on their social security; is this income redistribution?

The original concept by Roosevelt which in essence forced workers to put a little money into a program so they could support themselves in their old age, I believe was a good idea. There are many Americans that don't save a penny for their old age and indeed would live in poverty or those that did save would have to support them.

While I support the concept, I totally disagree with the government handling of the program. Over the years the program has been turned into a socialist welfare and insurance program at a cost that can't be sustained and benefits that are pitiful when compared to what was paid in.

It is estimated that forty million elderly would live in poverty if it weren't for social security which is totally believable, but that's only half the story. Some of those 40 million would indeed be living in poverty because they would not have saved. Those that would have saved would be much better off with a higher standard of living. Most social security recipients just don't realize what a rip off the program is.

The ultimate socialist part of social security is how they calculate benefits. Remember I said the socialist's want to redistribute wealth and the social security system has been doing that for years.

If you assume that a worker making an average of $45,000 a year and pays 6.2% or $2790 a year in social security makes half the benefits of a person making $90,000 a year, you will be wrong! The person making $45,000 will get max benefits of about 43% of his income while the person making $90,000 will get about 29% of his income.

How can it be when a worker pays twice the money into social security that he doesn't get twice the benefits? The formula for calculating benefits gives both workers about 44% credit up to $45,000 but everything above that figure only gets 15% credit because they use the payments from the higher income worker to increase the benefits for the lower income worker; thus, socialism and redistribution of wealth.

When you listen to the Democrats discuss how great the social security system is and explain how many of the elderly could not get by without it, consider this. I calculated that if the government had allowed me to invest in the stock market; not in one stock but the Dow Jones Industrial Average, allowing for all the ups and downs of the market, I would have been a multimillionaire. This would have provided me with an annual income many times my social security. Withdrawal could have been limited to equal yearly amounts base on the actuary tables used for required withdrawals from an IRA or 401K.

The Democrats claim it is too risky to invest Social Security in the stock market and seniors could end up broke; try asking them how many of you have investments in stocks or bonds and you will discover that almost every one of them does. Wouldn't that make them too stupid to run the country?; investing their money in something that they could go broke.

For those of you on social security that the government has convinced that it is the greatest thing since sliced bread, you better hang on to your hats because the following figures may change your mind.

A person making $90,000 a year pays $11,160 into social security; half from his paycheck and the other half from his benefits; remember even though his employer pays, it still comes out of his total pay and benefits package. Assuming he started working at the age of 25 and retired at 65, he would have paid $446,400 into social security.

The stock market has averaged a 10% return over the years and this takes into account the highs and the lows. If the $11,160 per year had been invested in the market, at age 65 you would have about 5.5 million dollars; that's right, 5.5 million! With a 4% return you would have an income of $220,000 per year. Does Social security still look like a good investment? By the way; the 5.5 million is almost 2 million more than the person made in total salary received in the 40 years. Welcome to The wonderful world of compounding.

So what if you only made a 5% return for those 40 years, half of what the stock market averaged? You would have to get by on only $110,000 a year

The person making $45,000 a year would of course make half the return since they paid half the investment but would still end up with over 2.75 million dollars and an income of $110,000 a year.

Nobody with any financial sense would ever invest their money in social security. Your government loves it because they are able to give part of the money you pay in for many years to those making less and socialist programs that pay for college and benefits to multiple spouses. Oh don't forget the fact that while they are doing all these things with your social security monies. There is none! There is no money in the fund as it was robbed years ago. This means there was no compounding of interest, in fact, no interest.

If you are on social security you get your check from those who are currently working. This means their money is not going into a fund and they will receive their social security from their children. Since young people are having less children how will they be able to pay enough into social security to pay their parents?

Medicare garners 1.45% of your income every year and never ends no matter how much you make. A person making $500,000 pays 10 times as much per year than someone making $50,000. I doubt that the higher earner will require 10 times the medical help in their senior years.

Let's look at the great investment in Medicare. The government will of course tell you what a great deal it is for seniors. Since my wife and I are on Medicare let's see if they are right or is it like social security; the worse investment know to man.

We'll use the person making $90,000 a year. They pay 1.45% or $1,305 a year. Again, their employer must match so the total is $2,610 a year. The total paid in 40 years is $52,200; remember we are buying a government insurance policy that won't take effect until age 65.

Using the stock market return, if we invested the money, when we reached age 65 we would have $1,271,000. Now which would you rather have, Medicare which covers only 80% of your medical expenses and you have to buy supplemental insurance to cover the other 20%; and don't forget they deduct a co-pay for part B from your social security check, or the $ 1,271,000?

If this doesn't convince you that government programs literally rob you; then think about this; if you die in a car crash or in any other manner, before you reach 65, all of the money you paid into social security and Medicare is lost. What a deal! On the other hand, if you had invested it, your heirs would be left a multimillion dollar estate

After paying all that money into Medicare for over 40 years, Medicare now pays 80% of doctors and hospital charges but the government takes over 100.00 a month out of your Social Security check for your part B premiums. You still need A supplement insurance plan to cover the 20 % the Medicare doesn't pay and that costs about $250.00 a month. You still don't have a prescription coverage so congress added part D to cover some of the cost but you have to pay about $60.00 a month out of your Social Security check and you will still have co-pays for your proscriptions. After paying into Medicare for about 40 years, if you don't die before reaching age 65 where you lose all the money you payed in, it will still cost you about $5000.00 a year above what Medicare will pay.

Both state and federal tax systems are socialistic in their structure. Low income people pay nothing and the higher your income the higher the percentage you pay. If a person made twice the income and the tax rates were the same they would pay twice the tax even though the benefits they receive are the same as the lower income; however, they are not charged the same rate, and may pay 5 or 6 times as much tax. By charging higher income workers a higher rate, it's income redistribution.

In spite of the many socialist programs we have in America, it's nothing to the programs that Obama wanted the government to get involved in. It appears to me that the trend in America since the great depression has been to try and socialize the country like Europe, except the Obama administration wanted it to happen today

Now that Donald Trump is president, he has reversed many of the programs instituted by the Obama administration and the country is turning around. The economy is great, unemployment at a 50 year low, and regulations that were killing our economy, cancelled. In spite of this, it was reported that 33% of college students have a favorable view of socialism; they must have formed this view from their far left professors and failed to follow the news that over 100.000 from Venezuela have crossed over the border to Columbia in search of food and medicine; Thousands more entering Guyana so they closed their border. Is this the socialism they want?

It's interesting to note, that our country was founded and formed mainly by Europeans who hoped to form a better country then they immigrated from, and they were truly successful. Now we are moving back to the ways of the countries our ancestors left. It's not uncommon for politicians to refer to how Europe does this or that. Since we are more powerful, more influential, and have a higher standard of living than Europe, why would we want to go back to doing things their way?

CHAPTER 8

Moral Decline

Pesident Trump or any other politician can't do anything about moral decline because you can't legislate morals which is evident from the failure of prohibition.

Socialism is devastating to a country's economy and standard of living as I am afraid we are about to discover, but even worse is a moral decline. A country can still survive with less money and less things if they still retain their values and morals.

If you think the capitalistic free enterprise system has experienced change from the days of our founding fathers, take a close look at how we live our lives and you will discover change that a senior citizen like myself, can hardly believe.

In my introduction I pointed out the fact that it was the moral decline that caused God to remove his helping hand from the Jews, but the final blow was their rejection of Jesus and as I stated, they have never truly recovered. Are we in the process of repeating that grave mistake?

There will be those who will claim that a belief in God is not necessary to live a good life; but they deceive themselves; Even if you believe in doing the right things, as humans, we are not capable of carrying them out without God's help. The temptations of the world and our own

47

sin nature often times overwhelm us. We won't get into Satan and his influence, but it's present.

I have read the Bible twice and have come to this conclusion; God started with man with only one rule and they failed. He then flooded the world because of man's sinful nature saving only a few. Next came Moses and God decided to write down how he wanted man to live, and again, they failed.

I believe that God came to the conclusion that man could not live the life he required without help from the Holy Spirit which we now have if we accept Jesus Christ. There is nothing to indicate there will be anymore effort by God then what he has provided. The world needs to understand; it's now or never!

It breaks my heart to see America following the same path as other one time great empires such as Greece and the Roman Empire. You can see what happened to both of them... How often do you hear anything of Greece except recently they were so much in debt that the EU (European Union) had to loan them money. Tourism keeps them going because of their History. Italy on the other hand stays more in the limelight because of the Vatican and the publicity it gets; lately not too positive!

What happened to these once great Empires? I believe the same thing that's happening today in America; a loss of values, principles, morals and most important of all, Godliness.

I believe the churches are a measuring stick for the moral well being of any country. It's not only how many attend church, which is certainly a critical factor, but what the churches teach those that do attend and finally, how they apply what they have been taught to the way they live their lives.

The person that attends church regularly receives reminders of God's will for our lives and this constant reminder will help us to stay on the right track; but in the end, hearing the word without a personal relationship with the Lord, is only a temporary fix and it doesn't work all the time; the result is that it is hard to tell the difference between many of the people that attend church and one who does not. The person who is a born again Christian has undergone a heart transplant; not physically, but spiritually.

If you look at church attendance statistics for countries in Europe you find most falls in the single digit range and America is quickly following suit.

The Southern Baptist Convention some years ago stated that for adults under the age of 23; only 4% attended church on a regular basis.

Frank Page, a former president of the SBC stated if the current trends in church membership and baptisms continue; half of the Southern Baptist churches will have to close their doors permanently by the year 2030. I use the Southern Baptist which has a membership of about sixteen million as an example mainly because they generally represent conservative biblical principles concerning morality, but other protestant denominations as well as the Catholic Church are also in decline.

It's such a wonderful feeling not to have to be "political correct" so you are able to write what you believe to be the truth. Politically correct means you must avoid any subject that might be controversial, and if you can't, just walk around the truth. If you get caught between a rock and a hard spot; just lie; we had seen a lot of that from people in the Obama administration or in a real pinch, take the fifth.

It is my belief, and experience. That we have become an entire society that rejects controversy. We don't like confrontation. Therefore, we never fix the problems. I once visited a church at the time the Southern Baptist Convention was about to split between the Liberal and conservative groups and I ask which way this church believed; their response was, we don't like controversy. We didn't go back. I thought how different things would be if Jesus and his disciples had felt that way since stoning, crucifixion, and beheading could certainly be considered confrontational.

Jesus and his disciples knew their stand was extremely controversial and they risked far more than we do today; by taking that risk, they changed the world forever. Standing up for the truth when the truth, as it still is today, was so unpopular, cost all but John who was exiled to the island of Patmos, their lives.

My wife and I have been members of Baptist churches since the early 70's. We chose the Baptists over other denominations for one basic reason; they believed the Bible was the perfect word of God and preach God's morals, values and how we are to live our life as Jesus has instructed us.

Their main fault is that they sometimes like to add additional restrictions that are not necessarily biblical. I sometimes believe they think if God put restrictions on certain things, wouldn't it better if we restricted them completely.

It took the Baptists a few centuries to finally admit that Jesus and his disciples drank wine. The church had always maintained that it was grape juice. I tried to reconcile their belief with statements in the Bible like: Jesus turned the water into wine at a wedding, and How about the Pharisees criticizing Jesus and his disciples for being wine drinkers. I can't imagine the Pharisees criticizing them for drinking Welsh's grape juice. I'm afraid this just didn't make sense. As I said, they now admit it was wine, therefore, you might assume the church preaches that wine or any alcoholic beverage, should be consumed according to the bible; not so.

Remember we are talking about conservative Baptist Churches not the more liberal branch. You will have a hard time finding a conservative Baptist church that would ever tell you it's ok to drink in moderation.

So why don't they follow the word of God when it comes to drinking when they faithfully follow most everything else? I have to believe that they are so against drinking because of the potential problems that they can't bring themselves to endorse the right of a Christian to drink responsibly according to the word.

I am sure that if no one drank, the world would be better off because of the abusers of alcohol. In this case the Baptists are expanding on God's word to improve things but there are in my opinion, two problems with this; we are instructed not to change one thing contained in the Bible, and when people hear their teaching and compare it to God's word, they may start to question other teachings. How then do Baptists justify telling people they shouldn't drink?

Paul who wrote many books of the New Testament, Made statements concerning the fact he wouldn't do things that might offend his brother while pointing out that it was lawful to do it. Using these passages to say you shouldn't drink at all leaves the door wide open to eliminating almost everything in life as I am confident I could find enough brothers somewhere that would be offended by most everything we do, are we therefore to stop living?

Why when a deacon is ordained do we read the passage in Timothy that describes how a deacon should conduct himself that states he should not be given to MUCH wine; do we then change it in practice and say NO wine?

I can tell you with certainty; I have never had a Baptist pastor give a sermon around the passage in the bible where the Pharisees criticize Jesus and his disciples for drinking wine and Jesus reminds them they criticized John the Baptist who didn't drink strong drink and Jesus for drinking wine. Keeping in mind the Pharisees were the religious leaders at that time. When the religious leaders of the Baptist denomination tell their members they shouldn't drink; are they not doing the same thing?

Their argument is you may cause a weaker Christian to stumble thus becoming a stumbling block; if this is true, Jesus and his disciples must have been the worse stumbling block for his followers, for who could be more in the limelight then they were.

If Jesus and some of his disciples were to come down to earth tomorrow like the angles did to check up on Sodom and Gomorra; and during their stay sat down to a meal with wine; would any pastor tell them they were being a stumbling block?

I know that their intention is good and is not like churches that justify sin. But there is an old saying (actually I don't know how old it is) that the road to Hell is paved with good intentions! Remember the results of prohibition?

The more liberal protestant churches ignore biblical truths to fit in with modern society. Anytime a church attempts to fit in or please society, there is no way they can please God. There is one major advantage to ignoring the more controversial statements in the Bible; the church will grow in attendance because the people don't want to hear the "thou shall not" rules from God.

Liberal churches have started to accept homosexuality in spite of the fact the Bible condemns such conduct as an abomination in the eyes of God. The Episcopalians and lately the Lutherans have even accepted practicing homosexual Pastors.

The people are not without blame, because they want to fit in with, and live like, the world and these pastors will claim the bible was written by men and therefore does not just contain God's word. The tricky part is determining which passages are gods, and which are mans. I suppose the best rule of thumb would be; if I don't agree with something in the bible, especially if it condemns or restricts, I determine that passage must have been written by man.

When I grew up in Flint, most of my friends that had church affiliation were Catholic. Flint was a manufacturing town and most Europeans involved in manufacturing were catholic. Contrast this with the south which was mainly agriculture, and they were mainly of the protestant faith.

The Catholic Church practices concern me the most because they were devised by man and did not originate from the Bible. Let's take the idea of purgatory, which is supposed to be a place between Heaven and Hell. If your loved one or relative ends up in purgatory, you can request mass to help them on to Heaven. Years ago you could request a low or high mass; of course the high mass cost more. There is no purgatory in the bible and paying for prayers certainly doesn't sound very Christian. Priests can't forgive your sins nor saying Hail Mary or counting beads; God is the only one who can forgive our sins. Praying to Mary because we're not worthy to pray to God, more man made rules because Jesus told us how to pray to the father. Consecrated ground to be buried in; where did this come from? If you get divorced you can't take the sacraments or be buried in consecrated ground; all man made rules.

I remember when Senator Kennedy wanted to divorce his wife of many years but to avoid the losses in the church practices of a divorced man requested from the Pope an annulment which was granted. They had two teenage sons which his wife Joan made a comment to the effect; will I tell my sons we were never married?

I think it was in the late 80's that a couple that I worked with asked my wife and me to attend a Bible Study at the Catholic Church... This was something new as the Catholic Church had always discouraged their parishioners from reading the Bible; it was too complicated for them to understand. The church would interpret it for them. I have a real problem with the idea that God would have his word written in such a way that his children couldn't understand it. Would you buy a car or house from a salesman who said, never mind reading the contract as its too complicated for you, just sign here? Isn't your soul more important?

The reason this couple wanted us to attend was because they knew we were Christians and wanted our opinion about the Bible Study; they had reservations about statements this priest would make.

There were many people attending the class and we were pleased that they were anxious to learn the word of God. The priest did not appear comfortable discussing the bible and during the lesson made the statement that the book of Job was not to be taking literally, but was more like a writing of Robert Frost. The Catholics held his feet to the fire and challenged him on several statements. They ask about being born again and when they brought up Satan, the priest was very uncomfortable.

I think that once many Catholics, especially the younger ones, started to read the Bible, they began to question many practices of their faith; some even leaving the church they grew up in, moving to other denominations.

Let's not forget to pick on the Catholic Church about The controversy over the homosexual abuse of small boys by priests that has now moved to the door of the Pope. Priests, who higher ups in the church knew were child molesters, simply moved them to another diocese where they continued their practice. This is unbelievable! This problem is finally being exposed as many states are demanding the records from the Catholic Church that identify the priests guilty of abusing little boys. The priests were not turned over to authorities for prosecution as anyone in society would be, but they just paid huge sums of money to the victims or their parents.

The Church doesn't allow priests to marry, perhaps because of a statement by Paul that it's better if you don't marry because your time and attention has to be divided between serving God and your family.

He concludes his statement saying if you can go without sex, this is fine, but if you can't control this, it's better to marry than to burn! I once had a pastor that added the words "with passion" after burn which changed the meaning from damnation to over excited, could this have been because there are so many living together or their children are that he didn't want to risk offending them?

It's apparent that some of the priests have failed and in a big way. I wonder why when they fail, they choose little boys and have a homosexual relationship rather than a normal heterosexual one with women. Is the Catholic Church attracting homosexual men to the priesthood?

I once questioned a catholic couple about how they felt having their donated money to do God's work having to be paid to abused boys and their families. At that time the church was expected to have to pay five hundred million dollars and by the time it ends, another five hundred million, where does a church get that kind of money? It is difficult for a person who has been raised in a particular denomination to leave when the practices of their church are not right but this is what they should do if the church refuses to change.

Remember when President Nixon had to resign or be impeached, not because he approved the Watergate break-in. But he covered up to prevent possible damage to the Republican Party. Popes can't be removed for any reason. This might be time for major changes in the Catholic Church and this will only happen if the parishioners rise up and demand the changes needed to have the Catholic Church follow Biblical guidelines. The idea that a Pope is infallible is not only ridiculous but contradicts the statement by Jesus when addressed as good master, responded why do you call me good, only the father is good.

There is a passage in chapter 7 in the book of Matthew where Jesus states that in the end days there will be those that come up to him saying; didn't we preach in your name, and heal in your name, and cast out demons in your name?; and I will say to them. Get away from me, ye that work sin, for I never knew you. I wonder if the pastors and priests of these churches that ignore God's word ever wonder if that saying might apply to them since most lay persons don't perform these duties.

Europe not only has just about abandoned church attendance, but a recent survey which ask how important is your relationship to God; the percentage of people that said it was important, matched the church attendance which is in single digits.

In France, a recent survey shows that 44% of the people don't even believe in God.

Homosexuality, living together while not being married and having children out of wedlock is pretty much accepted in Europe and we are heading in the same direction and in fact, may have already arrived.

As I write this, I try to visualize being able to travel back in time to the 1950's and explain to the people the way the people would be thinking, acting and living in 2014 and my first thought was; they would have me committed. In the 50's you could have people committed without proving they were a danger to themselves or to others. I feel confident society would think I had lost my mind to believe such nonsense.

Hollywood movies show such conduct as ok and many of the Hollywood crowd lives that way. Young people are influenced by Hollywood and the parents allow them to see these movies at an early age so why be surprised when they think and act the same way?

The music that young people listen to today is as bad as or worse than the movies. The language is filthy and violent and the live performances can be indecent; they make the gyrations of Elvis Presley appear tame; again I ask; where are the parents? Are their parents not aware of the content of the movies and music, which is hard to believe; or do they just not see anything wrong with it?

The thing that convinces me how far gone we are in America is the state of our churches. I have to emphasize again, when I refer to churches, I mean the people; and when the people start to tolerate ungodly conduct, even if they don't live that way themselves, we're definitely on a downhill slide.

If Christians knew what percentage of pastors does not believe in God; they would be shocked. How then can they preach from the bible? If there is no God, then there couldn't be God's word (the bible). Many pastors say it provides an income and they just tell the people what they want to hear. I suppose logically, if a person doesn't believe there is a God, then he wouldn't have a problem telling the flock that he does; who is going to hold him accountable?

A survey of pastors indicates the main reason they became pastors when they don't believe in God, is income. In the early days a pastor had to live on a shoestring as their pay was lower than any profession in the country.

Because of the low pay, a congregation could be pretty sure their pastor was a man called by God to minister to his flock. Often time's pastors were paid for their services with a chicken or vegetables.

Things began to change as churches started to pay their pastors more; they added benefits and soon pastors were making average incomes. I believe this was good as we should not expect a pastor and his family to live in poverty.

The problems started showing up when churches started paying above average incomes which attracted people into the ministry, not because they were called by God, but they felt they could make better money and they like the idea that they are pretty much their own boss.

The median income in 2014 for a person in a secular job with bachelor degree is $50,944 and according to recent survey of churches, the average senior pastor makes more than $80,000 in pay and benefits. The average pay scale based on church attendance is; 101-300 $72,664; 301-500 $88,502 and 501-750 makes $102,623. They are no longer being paid with chickens and these pay scales are not chicken feed.

If you were to ask most Christians they would tell you, pastors are worth much more than that; but that is not the point. Jesus instructed his disciples, if they had more than one coat, take only one with you. Jesus knew there needs would be met (notice I said needs, not wants). Jesus also knew that by having his disciples live a very modest lifestyle, the people could not fault them and accuse them of being money hungry, Paul worked as a tentmaker rather than be a financial burden on the church.

The important thing is for the church leader not to come across as a person more interested in money than serving God. I believe many pastors as well as the church members have started to think of the job of pastor like a secular position; nothing could be further from the truth.

The position of pastor by its very nature requires sacrifice and that has to include standard of living; it is to be a calling, not a profession.

My wife and I were living at the coast of North Carolina from 1998 to 2004 and during that time the Episcopal Church ordained a practicing homosexual as a Bishop which caused considerable controversy both within and without the Episcopal Church. A pastor of a large Baptist Church in Jacksonville wrote an article every Sunday for the local newspaper and condemned the ordaining of a homosexual because homosexuality is a sin in the bible; not only a sin, but an abomination in the eyes of God. It is also said no homosexual will enter heaven. If a Christian requires further proof, consider the fact that all the people in Sodom and Gomorra were destroyed by God because of their sinful lifestyles. I'm sure their sins were many, but the only one God saw fit to mention was homosexuality.

A member of an Episcopal Church wrote to the editor, criticizing the Baptist pastor. He went on to point out that there were Baptists that supported homosexuals and that homosexuals contributed to society. He stated the bible was written by man so not all of the word was from God.

I had never written to the editor before but somehow felt compelled to respond. I pointed out that denominations had nothing to do with the issue at hand. I was sure there were people from all denominations that would agree with him. The real issue is the bible.

I stated that I had heard this argument for years but it made no sense at all. First of all, no one has ever taken it upon themselves to rewrite the bible, leaving out all the sayings of man, and having only God's word remain: and who would be so arrogant to feel they were up to that task? If you can't separate God's word from men, what possible use is the bible to anyone? Finally, we have thousands of books written by man and they all contain the exact words they want them to, but God, who created the universe is not capable of having his word written as he wanted it to be. If you believe this, then you have to believe that man is capable of doing something that God can't.

As for Homosexuals contributing to society; what has that to do with anything?

God doesn't care about our contributions to society, he cares about our living our life as he has instructed.

The only reason this person or any person rejects parts of the bible as written by man not by God, is because they disagree with God on certain issues, such as lifestyles, punishment and Hell. In the end it really doesn't matter if we agree or disagree with God for it will be done his way.

I've listened to the scientists ramble on about how the universe was created since most do not accept the creationist theory where the bible merely says, God created everything. I suppose if they accepted that there wouldn't be much purpose to their profession.

Science has been prone to accepting the evolution theory where everything just sort of happened by chance or accident if you wish. God was not a consideration, but that may be changing with the discovery of DNA. It is said that the human DNA is so complex that if placed end to end, would reach to the moon. Scientists now are saying DNA that complex could not have happened by chance; so what then; could it be God; no it's intelligent design. It was reported that one scientist stated if there is a God he wouldn't have rules for people to live by.

That's exactly the way the majority of Americans feel, they don't want God or anyone else for that matter telling them how to live. They have rebellious hearts, and God in his evaluation of a person, looks at their heart.

There is a modern day saying by both purported Christians and non Christians alike; UNCONDITIONAL LOVE! Just to set the record straight, the word unconditional is never mentioned in the bible. People use this statement when referring to God's love. If it isn't in the bible, where did they come up with idea? The only thing I can figure out, is the biblical statement that "while we were yet sinners, Jesus loved us" and this is true, but you can't convert this to mean what people want it to mean. What people want this to mean, is that no matter how sinful you are, God loves you and won't punish you with Hell.

Here is a good example of how the term unconditional love is used: Tarleton State University in Texas allowed the 1998 play Corpus Christi to be performed which depicts a gay Jesus performing a same sex wedding for two of his gay Apostles. The Apostles are all gay and Joseph, Mary's husband, is a wife beater.

The play is being put on by a 26 year old student director as a class project to help bring people together and help gain acceptance for gay Christians. He stated "I want us all to know that UNCONDITIONAL LOVE means just that—UNCONDITIONAL.

There are no gay Christians, only those that claim to be. To be a Christian, we are to be Christ like, not just believe that he is. I guess by putting on this play where Christ is gay, they can now say; see, we are Christ like; what a sick world!

I ask a pastor one time, what percentage of people attending church do you think are really "Born Again Christians"; I then said I think maybe 20% and that could be on the high side. He responded by saying, Billy Graham once said that and received all kinds of flack.

Being born again means the person not only believes that Jesus is who he says he is but that you are turning your life over to him, and with the power of the Holy Spirit, be obedient to God's laws. It has no value to believe in Jesus without being born again. Jesus stated "you say you believe in God, that's good, but so do the Demons and they shudder" Jesus also told Nicodemus the Pharisee, you must be born again to enter the kingdom of God.

Looking at church attendance as a measure of a society's spiritual health can be very misleading. If they are not born again, then their attitudes and conduct will more closely mirror secular society than it would biblical principles. You know something is wrong when you are unable to tell the difference between a person claiming to be a Christian and an agnostic or atheist.

It is not uncommon to find a person that attends church regularly who has a son or daughter that is living with their girlfriend or boyfriend and the parents accept this situation rather than condemn it. When ask why they are not taking a Christian stand, they will respond; I couldn't do that; what they should have said is I wouldn't do that. The result is their children never change; in fact, they become arrogant and rebellious and flaunt their sin publicly without shame.

I was watching Wheel of Fortune on TV and one of the contestants, a woman, stated she had been married five years and they had three children with the oldest being eight. She had no problem letting the millions of viewers know she had been living with her now husband for several years before they were married and had an illegitimate child with him.

If we don't believe in the bible which instructs us how we are to live, then what is sin? Who will define sin? Will it be determined by what is socially acceptable? Isn't that what is happening in our country today?

We have Co-ed dorms where the parents have no problem with their son or daughter having sex without being married. Drinking underage and the parents provide the alcohol even though it's against the law. I had one mother I knew that provided alcohol to high school kids that were friends of her son but she made them give her their car keys so they wouldn't drive; I suppose keeping them from killing someone solved the whole problem. I guess encouraging teens to break the law if you don't agree with it didn't seem like a problem. Will the parents take responsibility if one day their son goes to jail for dealing drugs when he tells them he didn't agree with the drug laws so he did the same thing his parents did about the alcohol. Maybe taking their car keys was more of a self protection that a concern for others. If they were in an accident that injured or killed someone, the police would want to know where they got the alcohol. Even if they didn't get jail time, the door would be open for civil lawsuits.

Throughout this book I keep harping on a lack of accountability. Not long before the situation I just mentioned, the wife of a Governor was charged with providing alcohol to minors but never served one day in jail so why should any parent worry about being caught? I say this because they don't seem a bit concerned that the teens may become an alcoholic or die from binge drinking.

The Governor of Maryland and his wife a District judge felt it was just a family problem when there eighteen year old daughter was found by police unconscious from alcohol poisoning. Police requested an ambulance. The next day the judge issued a statement indicating her daughter had attended a graduation party before she became ill and had to receive medical treatment. She said it was a teachable moment. There was nothing said about alcohol abuse by a minor. The daughter wasn't charged so where is her accountability? What kind of parents doesn't know what kind of party their daughter will be attending? Where is their accountability? Who provided alcohol to a minor and where is their accountability?

Wow! What an example our political leaders are for America, not only by their irresponsible conduct; but the fact no one is held responsible.

One thing that stood out as an example of the lack of morals of the American people, was when then President Bill Clinton attended church on an Easter Sunday clutching his little bible like any good Christian should. Easter being the holiest day of the year for Christians as we celebrate the resurrection of Jesus from the dead; it's not surprising to see the President attending church: I was surprised when later we found out he went straight home to the Whitehouse from church to have sex with the young intern.

Now you would think the average American regardless of political affiliation would be terribly offended by the President's actions, but they were not. Wasn't it bad enough that the President of the United States was having sex in the white house with a person not his wife; but what a hypocrite, to appear on TV to be worshiping God.

If you think I'm surprised or shocked that Bill Clinton would do this, you would be wrong. Bill has been committing adultery on his wife for many years by his own words to Monica Lewinsky. What then is surprising? I believe if Clinton could have run for a third term, he would have been elected! Doesn't this show that the average American doesn't have any better morals than the former President?

You had to notice that Hillary Clinton defended Bill claiming a right wing conspiracy was the problem, and when positive DNA evidence showed it was true about her husband, she never apologized for the false accusations. Hillary had to know Bill was running around with everything that wore a skirt but stayed with him. Why would she do that? It's not like a one time error of judgment: he was a full time runner.

I believe she loved the limelight of politics so much she was willing to stay with the person she thought could catapult her into the Whitehouse; how sad for Hillary. In the end she lost to Obama. Perhaps the people had a more difficult time with her handling of the situation, than with Bill's infidelity. What a world!

After losing to Obama she decides to run again and this time the Democratic Party was in full support; it appeared Hillary was a shoe in. but she has opposition from a socialist, Bernie Sanders. It now appears socialism is already starting but Hillary was able to crush the Bernie campaign and now she felt there is no way she would be defeated especially when a non- politician by the name of Trump had won the Republican nomination. He had never ran for office before and now was trying to be President of the United States. Trump calls her crooked Hillary and who would have suspected that the emails from her closest advisers would be hacked and released to the public. Those emails showed that her own people believed that Hillary didn't always tell the truth. I guess Trump hit the nail right on the head. It may be possible that GOD wanted Hillary to be exposed for the good of the wonderful country he had given to the Christians.

Hillary is pitiful, she can't accept that her lack of any plan for the country other than we will build 500 million solar panels while we put the coal and steel workers out of work was absurd. She still to this day can't accept that she was a poor candidate with no ability to talk to the people. It appears she thought she had no competition in Trump so she didn't need to have a plan to help the people.

CHAPTER 9

The Blind Leading the Blind

How can it be that people in the United States appear to be so uninformed and completely blind to the truth and the facts? By being blind, they keep on living the way they have, not realizing or perhaps not accepting what the end results is bound to be.

In Matthew Chapter 15, Jesus refers to the religious leaders, the Pharisees and their followers as the blind leading the blind and when this happens they both fall in the ditch. The Pharisees were distorting the word of God and most of the people followed them. Isn't that what's happening today?

Many churches are distorting the bible and the people follow, but it's not just the churches as we already mentioned, less and less people attend church, so where do they get their information?

We already know that young people are influenced by Hollywood and the music world; both which endorse, and live, lifestyles that offend God: they not only offend God, but have disastrous results. The entertainment industry is notorious for drug use, free sex, multiple marriages and divorces, alcoholism, and homosexuality. We see the impact of their influence on our youth more and more every day. Look how many in the entertainment business have died young from drugs and suicide.

What about the adult population; what influences them? Most adults would say, nothing and nobody influences me, I'm my own person and make my own decisions. If we are not influenced by what we hear, then how did Adolph Hitler convince so many youth to turn in their own parents that disagreed with the Nazi Agenda? Their parents were executed or sent to concentration camps. How did a raving maniac manage to get elected by the people in the first place?

Jim Jones, religious leader of the Peoples Temple, a religious cult, talked over 900 followers in Guyana to either commit suicide or they were murdered. This cult was supported by President Carter and his wife, the Board of supervisors in San Francisco and many more supposedly well educated individuals. Do you think they were influenced by the words of an evil man?

David koresh and the Cult Branch Davidians in Waco Texas all died in the FBI raid. Almost 80 people followed the 9th grade dropout. David considered himself an angel of God and some of his worshipers thought he was God incarnate. Imagine an uneducated man who originally wanted to be a rock star was able to influence the people to the point it cost them their lives.

In the late 60's I dabbled a bit with hypnosis and while it was unbelievably fascinating, it was at the same time a bit scary. With nothing but words, you could convince a person to do or say almost anything.

I read several books by professors that studied hypnosis to try and better understand how it works and possible good applications. In one of the books the writer told of a Doctor during the Civil War that amputated over 500 limbs without anesthesia using hypnosis.

I found it to be true, that you could control a person's pain, hearing, sight, and smell with nothing more than words. Hypnosis proves that the mind controls almost everything in the human body.

I will give you one example of my experience that I found to a bit mind boggling; my wife and I were going to her sister's house and I decided to try a post hypnotic suggestion on my wife who worked with me. I told her when she saw her sister she would run up to her and say; sister, I just heard the most exciting thing and I want to share it with you;

she was to then recite "Mary Had a Little Lamb" To make it more of a challenge, I told her when she woke, she would remember everything.

My wife now knew what I had told her she would do. She was wide awake and on the way to her sister's house, argued with me that it was ridicules, and just because I told her to do it didn't mean she had to. I responded by telling her, of course you will. When we were almost there, she tried to rationalize by saying she didn't have to do that but would for me. I told her no, you won't do it for me, but because you have to.

When we arrived at her sister's house, she tried for a few seconds to resist but finally gave in and followed my instructions; to say that her sister was flabbergasted is a gross understatement.

Don't tell me we are not influenced by what we hear from others.

Thoughts and ideas will pop up in our mind at the strangest times and places. The worse of these ideas are often placed there by nothing more than the words of a charismatic individual like the ones just mentioned.

The question that I can't get answered, is whether the individual was actually convinced by another, or did they already believe that way and welcomed the support by some one else.

A case in question occurred in the 1950's in Denmark where a local hypnotist had a grudge against a businessman. He had a college student, Palle Hadrup that he had worked with for some time that was an excellent subject. Not all people can be hypnotized and not at the same depth. Don't think only weak minded people can be hypnotized, because the exact opposite is the case. A retarded or insane person can rarely be hypnotized because it requires communication and concentration by the subject.

A person that can reach the point where they can see objects that don't exist or not see objects that do, is considered an excellent subject; this was the case with the college student.

The hypnotist told the student to go to the office of the person he had the grudge against and shoot him. The student was provided a gun where he proceeded to the man's place of business and emptied the gun into him.

When the case appeared in the court, the hypnotist was no problem as they sentenced him to life in prison; the real problem was what to do with the college student; was he responsible or was it out of his control?

Experts in hypnosis testified that they couldn't be sure if a person would perform an act against their will; there were those that thought they would, and those that disagreed. The court sentenced the student to five years, perhaps as a sort of compromise.

Keep in mind, this student killed a man he didn't even know, because he was told to. There were no mind altering drugs, just words! The unanswered question for the court was; would the student have killed the man, say, for money? Was the act really something he might do under other circumstances?

Hypnosis is an overt act of working to concentrate all of a person's senses to the voice of the hypnotist so that he gains control over your mind, but in the case of Hitler, Jones and koresh, they were able to sell their radical beliefs without the use of hypnosis.

Just like the court case in Denmark, the question remains, were these radical leaders really able to sell their ideas to unsuspecting souls, or did their followers really agree with their agenda from the get go?

Let's take the case of young people; I'm talking school and college age; I believe they are easily influenced by their teachers and professors because of two reasons; they are idealistic and want to resolve all the problems and injustice in the world; and they are rebellious against the establishment and their parents.

It is my belief that the very worse place a parent can send their child is to college. I say this because the vast majority of educators are very liberal and in many ways have never grown up. Most of us felt like the students of today, but with age became wise and we realized there were limits to what could be accomplished; with wisdom came common sense and reality. It appears that many of those that decided to become educators, for the most part never transitioned into full adulthood. They love teaching because they have the perfect forum and the perfect age in which to brainwash. They only present their distorted version of country, religion and values and you can see the results in today's young people.

The established adult population is another story completely. Assuming they have matured past the college age, where do they get the information and ideas that influence their decisions? The other question is; do they even want to know the facts and the truth or involved in decisions at all?

I find it unbelievable that about half of the eligible voters do not vote which means to me, they are willing to accept whatever decisions their elected representatives make even if it results in losing freedoms, paying higher taxes or supporting countries and their ways that the American people don't accept. There's not much point to discussing these individuals because they won't be able to change anything in our society and frankly don't seem to care. You will often hear these people state that it doesn't matter who you elect but this is a way of justifying shirking their responsibility. History has shown the differences that take place based on who is in office.

Let's look at the people that do vote and ultimately place the people in office that determine the direction our country will take. The big question that I have; is the average American qualified to vote? When I say qualified, I'm referring to knowledge of the issues; the history of politics in the United States and the impact both good and bad of those decisions and the possible impact of the individual or political party's platform could have on our country.

A survey not long ago found that about 1 out of every three people ask, did not know the name of the Vice President of the United States; if you think that's bad, 25% don't know what country we fought for our independence. If they don't know something that elementary, what could they possibly know about healthcare, taxes, finance, war, immigration, etc? Maybe they think, I don't want to get involved in those kinds of issues, I'll leave that up to the politicians; well we have, and what a mess! Something even scarier is a young man associated with Fox News went on the street asking people to sign a petition to revoke the 1st amendment to the constitution that guarantees individual rights and many of all ages signed it; wow!

Newspaper circulation decline I believe is due to two factors; technology and biased newspaper reporting. With few exceptions, anyone that depends on their local newspaper to provide them with unbiased facts will never be able to make an informed decision.

It's not necessary for a newspaper to outright lie to support their view when all they have to do is leave out some important facts that might lead you to a different conclusion then they prefer.

My Cousin recently sent an EMAIL that I'm going to use to make my point and it went something like this:

A young girl was at the Zoo with her parents and was leaning in toward the lion cage when the lion grabbed her collar to pull her into the cage. A man on a motorcycle saw what was happening and ran to her assistance. He punched the lion squarely on the nose and he released the girl's collar. A man approached the hero and said that was the bravest thing he had ever seen. He identified himself as a reporter with the Washington Post (a well known far left newspaper) and informed the man his exploit would appear on the front page of the newspaper the next day. The reporter then asks the man what he did for a living and what his political affiliation was. The hero responded that he was a Marine and a republican.

The next day the Marine decided to see if the reporter did as he said he would and there on the front page was the headline: MARINE ATTACKS AFRICAN IMMIGRANT AND STEALS HIS LUNCH. You will notice that everything in the headline was absolutely true but by the phrasing of the headline made you see the Marine as a scumbag instead of a hero.

Now this example may be a slight exaggeration (but I could be wrong) but it makes the point that we must know the source of our information and how reliable they are; notice that I didn't say how much we agree with them, but how much we can trust them to provide accurate, unbiased information; and in many cases both positions on a controversial subject.

I have become a firm believer and strong supporter of FOX NEWS. I believe they are the most reliable source of important happenings that every American needs to be aware of. This may be the only source for news where the blind leading the blind does not apply. Now I'm not claiming that the people that work for FOX don't have their personal beliefs as that would be ridiculous; we all have our personal beliefs.

What I really like about FOX is that they will cover an issue whether it is the economy, taxes, the war, healthcare, national debt or any other issue that's important to most Americans, and have people that represent both sides of the discussion to present their views for our consideration. I liked the way Bill O'reilly closed his discussions that presented both sides "we'll let the folks decide"

It's not that I have always agreed with Bill O'reilly; if I had to make a guess, I'd say about 80% of the time, but even then, it's straight talk and I like. On one of his programs, Bill had an atheist as a guest and they discussed religion; during that discussion Bill made the statement that he couldn't guarantee that Jesus was the Son of God but based on all the facts over time, it is most likely that he is.

This is exactly the statement I would have expected from Bill and the reason I say that is because he comes across to me as an intellectual and made the decision about Jesus as an intellectual. My being a Baptist Born Again Christian know that the only way you can have a personal relationship and firm belief in Jesus is not with the mind, but with the heart; only then can you say I know that Jesus is the Savior and the Son of God.

Another position that Bill and I would not agree on is his statement that homosexuals should be able to adopt children. The bible states that homosexuality is an abomination in the eyes of God. It also states that a homosexual will not enter Heaven. As I pointed out about Sodom and Gomorra, the only sin mentioned before God destroyed them, was homosexuality. I suppose if you don't really think the bible is the word of God, you can get around these statements. I wouldn't mind having a good discussion with Bill O'reilly on his beliefs.

I also watch Shaun Hannity which used to be Hannity and Combs. I feel compelled to make an observation about Allen Combs as a far left liberal. Allen always appeared to me to be a nice guy; so nice, that he couldn't find a person in the wrong or guilty no matter what the facts showed. I remember many times Shaun Hannity would try to get Allen to admit that a particular person had committed an act or crime they were accused of, and no matter how overwhelming the evidence, Allen just couldn't do it.

I once envisioned a scenario between Shaun and Allen going something like this:

Hannity, I think George is going to have the book thrown at him for killing that man. Combs, he's innocent until proven guilty.
Hannity, but there were five witnesses!
Combs, you know that eye witness testimony is not always reliable.
Hannity, but it was his gun.
Combs, doesn't prove he fired it.
Hannity, he had gunpowder residue on his hand!
Combs, he might have got that at the range.
Hannity, he took a polygraph test and failed!
Combs, they're not reliable and not admissible in court.
Hannity, He confessed!
Combs, police have been known to force false confessions before.

Bill O'reilly, we'll let the folks decide

As I said, Allen appears to be a nice guy and if I were guilty as sin of a crime, I would want Allen on my jury.

Getting back to Shaun Hannity, I don't always agree with his positions either. I think if we are perfectly honest, none of us has ever met anyone that we agree with 100% of the time. My wife and I have been married for 61 years and do not agree on many things. We hash over the facts as we see them and in the end most of the time retain our own convictions; there are times when by discussion of the facts we are able to influence the other's position.

One position of Shaun's that I opposed had to do with the Schiavo case where her husband wanted to remove her feeding tube after several Doctors said she was brain dead. Her parents claimed she looked right at them and they felt sure she knew them. This became a protracted court fight which the husband finally won.

During the battle Shaun and several others which I think included Bill O'reilly felt the parents should be able to keep her alive. The husband on the other hand said his wife told him she didn't want to be kept on life support if the doctors said there was no hope.

I opposed the parent's right to overstep the husband's decision based on the bible which says, for this cause a woman will leave her parents and cleave unto a husband. The day she married, her husband and she became as one, and the parent's responsibility is over.

The tube was removed and she died. The doctors had said they were as sure as they could be that she was brain dead but only an autopsy of the brain would prove that for sure. An autopsy was performed and they found that she could not have been looking at her parents because she was blind.

I criticized Hillary Clinton for accusing a right wing conspiracy for her husband's problem and then not apologizing when it proved to not be true so in all fairness I have to say that those that took the parent's side should have come out and said; while it's understandable, the parents were wrong, as she was brain dead with no hope of recovery. This might have taken the heat off the husband which it should have.

The former Fox warrior Glen Beck; now here is a man after my own heart! He is much more emotional than Bill O'reilly and Shaun Hannity and some people don't like that, but I feel that Glen is that emotional because he is so concerned with not only what has happened to America, but what he sees happening in the future. It is obvious he genuinely cares about his country and the people. His emotion is an effort to impress upon his viewers how serious our situation in America is. I have experienced the same criticism even from family members because they see it as anger instead of emotion.

God when he created us with our complex DNA, each different from the other gave us different personalities, likes and dislikes, and callings in life. Those callings apply to the work we do and the way we are to serve God.

When I look at Bill O'reilly, Glen Beck, and Shaun Hannity I see those differences.

Bill O'reilly was looking for justice in America and has done an outstanding job of bringing to the attention of the folks (as Bill would say), those in a position that their ideas and/or actions could or have a negative effect on the well being of our country.

He has exposed Activists judges that wanted to give unbelievably light sentences to pedophiles that have sexually abused little boys and girls. I remember one case where a judge was going to give six month probation for a man's third conviction. It was Bill O'reilly's bringing this travesty to the attention of the people that forced the judge to give the man a prison sentence. How many children did he save from the fate of those others?

How about that far left professor Ward Churchill, a professor at Colorado University making the statement that the victims of 9/11 were "little Eichmanns". This referred to Adolf Eichmann, the organizer of the holocaust in world war two. What parents would want their children to be brainwashed by a man like Ward Churchill?

Ward was eventually fired by the university, not for his horrible comments, but for plagiarism. If it had not been for O'reilly, Ward would most likely still be spewing his hateful rhetoric.

Doesn't it make you wonder how a professor could be teaching such doctrine to the students and the parents not overwhelming the university demanding his removal? They must not pay any attention to their education or they don't have any problem with his ranting. The last choice is; they don't want the confrontation so they convince themselves that his teaching won't have any impact on their son or daughter; if this is the case, they couldn't be more wrong. They will discover what the impact was when it's too late to intervene.

O'reilly has exposed others including politicians whose statements would have you believe they have a radical agenda outside the beliefs of mainstream America. This responsibility that Bill has taken on would have keep him and his staff working long hours because Obama had appointed more people with radical ideas then all the previous presidents combined going back to Franklin Roosevelt. It seems he only waned far left radicals or those incompetent to serve in the job he appoints them to. Sorry to see Bill go.

Glen Beck as I see him has a different purpose in life; he wants to show the American people what is happening in the country that will have consequences that will affect their lives in a very disturbing way. I believe his purpose is to convince his listeners that they must do something to stop what is happening.

I think that Glen knows if the people fail to rally and stop the madness that is taking place in our country today, we are going down the tubes! He covered the gauntlet of issues from debt to healthcare presenting the facts that the politicians don't want us to know.

He provided the statements made by the Obama appointees so you can see how radical they were and if they were able to implement their ideas, how devastating it would be for the people.

I believe the FOX news team played a major role in the Tea Party Movement by providing for the first time, honest information to the people that moved them to action. It's no wonder the far left hates them so.

I saw where Glen Beck had won first place on the hate list of the far left. I can only say congratulations! Obviously, Glen is doing a fantastic job of exposing their radical agenda for America. Let's not forget to give credit to others on their hate list which includes Sarah Palin at number 2, Bill O'rielly number 9. That makes two from Fox news in the top 10; sorry Shaun, you were number 12, if you want to move up, you have to attack more.

While O'reilly, Beck and Hannity all overlapped some in the issues they covered, as I said, they each have a little different goal and approach to our country's problems. Shaun appears to me to like to expose bad conduct and bad decisions of the politicians, Hollywood, and others. Like Bill and Glen, the far left were their primary targets because their ideas contradict the goals of our founding fathers. Like I stated previously, our founders created a Constitutional Republic while the far left wants to convert America to a socialist form of government. Shaun often tries to expose the hypocrisy of the Democrat Party especially when it comes to covering up or refusing to remove members of their party guilty of improper conduct. I do find it interesting when he tries to get a democrat to admit their party did not handle these situations properly. All I can say to Shaun is good luck!

Now the following statement is going to appear very judgmental and it probably is, but I believe for the most part, it's also very true; you can't count on most liberal democrats to use or apply the same standards as most conservatives. Notice I said most, since there are always exceptions to every rule; we have to look at the norm not the exception. Conservative people I believe are more likely to use Biblical principles and teachings when they make their decisions; while I also believe that most liberals seldom consult the Bible, and if they do, it will be in some convoluted way to support their personal belief. Remember it is the far left liberals that want prayer out of school; in God we trust off our money, under God out of the pledge. When I say to Shaun, good luck, it's because I don't believe any amount of discussion will ever change their minds.

I have stopped watching the major networks because I can't count on them to provide the truth. They are so biased to the left that they appear to have no problem distorting the facts to support their agenda. They not only will not provide their viewers with an opposing view; but if the facts support a position they don't agree with; you won't hear about it at all. Issues that are important to Americans will not be covered by these networks if they don't support the far left agenda. It is my true belief that if a person counts on the major networks for important information; it will be the blind leading the blind. I'm happy to see more and more people each day switching to FOX for reliable information. I would hope that the major networks would realize their error and change the way they report the news so we would have more than one news source, but everything I've seen indicates they are so committed to their far left agenda they will not change even if they continue to lose viewers. How sad!

When I talk about the blind leading the blind, it applies to both problems in America, moral and financial and they are so intertwined that each one affects the other.

The statement by Jesus applied to the moral or Godly aspect of life only and referred to people following religious leaders that were not right with God; in his case it was the Pharisees. Today it is churches that don't follow the bible and cults that have nothing to do with God except in some abstract way.

We have already talked about the fact that less and less people attend church and many churches are not Godly in their teachings; that parents not only do not require their children to live a moral life, but many parents don't as well. What's that old saying "monkey see, monkey do" Unless there is a great catastrophe (which may be just around the corner) that causes people to come running to God, there's no point to beat a dead horse about morals.

Let's look at the financial or economic well being of out Nation which I believe is about to collapse, big time!

Let's compare 1950 and how the average American operated financially with today and it isn't hard to see why we're in serious trouble.

Most families in 1950 lived on one income and credit cards were almost non existent. People generally lived within their means because they had to save their money until they had enough to pay cash for their purchases.

To borrow money from a bank almost required that you had the money in savings. The average conventional mortgage was about 14 years. The result was a person would save for a down payment on a small home that they could afford because the short length of the mortgage significantly increased their monthly payment.

In 1950 only 60% of households had a car and today the average is over 2 cars per household. It's not only the cost to purchase the cars but the maintenance, license plates, inspection insurance and let's not forget property tax.

Today we spend almost all of our income and then use credit cards to borrow on our future earnings. The average family savings account balance is $3800 which means if there is a job loss or sickness that causes a temporary loss of income or additional expenses; there's no money in the bank to cover them. The result often is bankruptcy. In 1950 with a population of 152 million, there were 18,500 bankruptcies while in

1991 with a population of 252 million, there were 943,987 bankruptcies. A 65 percent increase in population and a 5200 percent increase in bankruptcies.

Why don't the people today save for a rainy day like they did in 1950 and make an effort to live within their means? I believe there are three main reasons.

The first is that young people want to start out in life with everything their parents have accumulated after 30years. They aren't wiling to start small and gradually work their way up. In many cases they start out with more than their parents have. They buy larger houses, fancier cars, take more expensive vacations, cruises, and eat out more often and at better restaurants.

Their parents are mainly responsible for this attitude as they gave them everything when they were growing up; there was no requirement to work and earn their allowance. Parents provided expensive video games, new cars, and expensive clothes and take them on a cruise while still in high school. This is the lifestyle they became used to; is it any wonder they thought it should never end?

Even the children of parents who didn't lavish on them find they have started to think the same way because most of their friends have been spoiled rotten by their parents. It's hard to restrict your spending and go without things while all your friends don't. Again, we are influenced by others and their lifestyles whether we want to admit it or not.

The second reason is they think they are able to do this because both spouses work and buying on credit is so easy. Take that cruise and put it on the credit card, buy that 52 inch TV and put it on the credit card, eat out three nights this week and put it on the credit card, and on and on. If the financial institutions wouldn't loan money that easy, they wouldn't be over their head in debt. How does a person get so many credit cards with high limits that they end up maxing out followed by bankruptcy? The banks get such a high interest rate they are willing to gamble.

The third (and very worse reason) they spend and spend and don't save; they think when their parents die they will inherit a bunch of money which will replace the money they never saved. What about those old sayings (never count your chickens before they hatch) and (a bird in the hand is worth two in the bush).

A recent article indicated that those that counted on their inheritance to save them have had a real awakening because the average inheritance has been about $45,000. How long do you think you could live on that? The reasons they give for the small amount is twofold, parents are living longer and traveling more which depletes their savings.

Their children may well be living longer but it doesn't appear they will be doing much traveling or much else for that matter.

What about their pensions? Only about 10 percent of companies still offer pension plans that pay a defined amount and only about 30% invest in a 401K plan. For those that do invest in the plan; the balance in those plans today is $16,500 for those age 22 to 34, $63,600 age 35 to 48, $126,900 age 50 to 67. Since pensions are going the way of the dinosaur and about 70% of the people don't invest in an IRA or 401K plan, what's going to happen to them in their old age? They can't afford to put the maximum into their IRA/401K because they live high on the hog every day, living just for today and blind to the resultant realities of their old age.

Some experts say a baby boomer will need about one million dollars in a retirement plan; that's a far cry from the current median in their account of $17,000.

Statistics show that more than 40% of Americans have less than $500 in savings and for those 25 to 34 years old it's 55%. When an emergency arises like car trouble or you need a crown on a tooth, it's time to use the plastic again.

Many years ago I looked at the fact that most people were spending all their income plus borrowing on future income and thought; the economy is booming because of the amount of money each family is spending. We have full employment and things things, things!

I then applied a little grammar school math and said, when the families have charged all they can afford the monthly payments for; won't they have to stop spending? When they stop spending, won't the people that make the things, things, things get laid off from their jobs?

This could be their neighbors or it could be them. Does this scenario sound familiar to you?

If you think this is not a good scene, be patient, it gets worse!

Could there be a problem with the blind politicians leading the blind electorate? I've already mentioned that many Americans are really not qualified to vote, but since there are no qualifications other than age 18 and citizenship, they do vote; and vote they did in presidential election that President Obama won. I will be the first to admit that most often I vote republican but do on occasions vote for the democrat candidate. I look at their ideas, qualifications, and perceived integrity, and vote accordingly.

I didn't care that Obama was black or a Democrat; I only cared about his beliefs and programs and how they will affect not just myself, but the country and this has to be the very worse president since Jimmy Carter. I find it a bit ironic that for many years I found that the worse president in my lifetime was a white southern peanut farmer who has now moved to second place by a black northerner, I don't know what he did for a living president.

Obama's ideas are more in line with a former socialist leader like Chavez in Venezuela than a constitutional republic like America. Obama didn't really care what the majority of Americans want or believe and even less about the rule of law; he had his own agenda and that is all that was important to him making him a true left winger. They believe their ideas are so good and so right that it gives them the right to overrule their American constituents.

His ideas from all I have seen are truly from a blind man; he may not be physically blind but he definitely is blind to the truth. His healthcare program is nothing more than a welfare program; it didn't reduce costs but healthcare costs went up instead. Obama said you could keep your plan and your doctor which turned out to be false. People like me that are on Medicare will be shortchanged under the guise of eliminating fraud. Obama had appointed a man to be in charge of Medicare and Medicaid that has endorsed rationing and he admires the socialist healthcare system in England. Obama was doing this while the Congress was in recess so he could bypass Senate approval which was in doubt; what arrogance.

Healthcare is only one of many acts that show he was certainly blind to the will of the American people. Taking the state of Arizona to court claiming their new law concerning illegal immigrants is unconstitutional when the vast majority of Americans are in favor of the law.

Common sense should convince you that Obama really wanted to grant amnesty and full citizenship to the millions of illegal immigrants and had no real interest in securing the border. I believe he was so against stopping the flow of illegal immigration that he had attempted to stop the states from enforcing the law which the federal government has failed to do for decades. I am glad the courts had seen through the Obama administration lawsuit and ruled partially in favor of the states rights to look out for the safety and welfare of their people.

When Obama was running for President it was shown to the American people the kinds of people he associated with and they weren't very nice. William Ayers was a radical in the Weather Underground, a self proclaimed Communist Revolutionary group; a violent organization that bombed police stations and government buildings. Ayers would be in prison today if it were not for the illegal wiretaps of the Nixon administration which freed him on a technically. His statement was "guilty as hell and free as a bird, it's a great country" This man is now a professor at the University of Illinois at Chicago. As a parent, I can't imagine allowing one of my daughters to attend a University that would employ such a man. If they wanted to attend there, they would have needed a good job because their parents would not pay one penny. If parents refused to send their children to this University because of professors like Ayers, the University would have no choice but to replace him. This is just another example of parents that do nothing to ensure their children receive the proper education and don't become radicalized by professors like William Ayers and Ward Churchill.

Reverend Wright who professes to be a Christian pastor but who's ranting shows he has no knowledge of Jesus Christ, had been Obama's pastor for 20 years. Obama claimed he wasn't aware of Wright's radical preaching and the blind followers of our blind president accepted his statement. No reasonable person could possibly believe you could set in a church for twenty years and not know how your pastor believed and acted.

Maybe they weren't that blind but hungered for the change that Obama was promising so they overlooked his radical associations. Big mistake!

The news channels help them to accept his associations by saying its wrong to judge guilt by association. Geraldo Rivera on Fox news was also against the concept of guilt by association. What happened to those old sayings (a man is judged by the company he keeps) or (birds of a feather flock together)? Obama finally left the church but I don't believe it was for moral reasons but political.

Reverend Wright made the statement that President Obama threw him under the bus for his controversial statements while privately agreeing with him; yet his blind followers still supported him and didn't want to be confused by the facts.

The Gulf oil spill should have convinced all Americans regardless of political affiliation that Obama falls into one of two categories; incompetent, or an opportunist who let the BP Oil Company try to handle the spill by themselves without assistance from the administration hoping the spill would be bad enough he could stop drilling for oil. Obama had never favored drilling for oil and this offered the opportunity to shut down new attempts to find oil. He did set a six month moratorium on drilling but a Federal Court issued an injunction to his order.

President Trump has opened up new areas for oil and gas exploration and is considering more which will not only make us energy independent but stop the vast flow of American dollars to the Middle East. Whatever dollars that stay in our country only helps our economy.

A 90 year old law, the Jones act, which restricts foreign ships from operating within 3 nautical miles of our coast should have had a waiver issued right after the spill so other countries that offered assistance could cleanup oil close to shore, but it wasn't done. President Bush issued a waiver 4 days after hurricane Katrina.

The fact that Obama had turned down all help offered by other countries and not issued a waiver of the Jones Act while not proving his motive was to use this accident to put a stop to drilling for oil, it's more than a little suspicious. I will repeat that those with a far left ideology seem to believe their ideas are so right that any means to achieve them is acceptable.

How is it possible that President Obama didn't have an approval rating in the teens? Everything Obama endorses is either a failure or the exact opposite of the will of the American people, yet his approval rating was in the mid to upper 30's. This has to be a classic example of the blind leading the blind.

Maybe those that approved of Obama's presidency actually saw things as they really were but one of the most difficult things for all of us to do is admit when we were wrong. There was a bit of hope in the elections because no matter how a person answers polling questions, when they get in the voting booth they can cast their vote without anyone knowing the results.

The 2016 elections show how true this was. All of the polls and all of the pundits Predicted Hillary Clinton would be the next president. Then again maybe the reason the polls were so wrong when they are normally quite accurate, is because politics has become so nasty especially from the democrats and their followers, the voters don't want to reveal their political leanings.

I saw a poll that showed about 55% of likely voters now believe Obama is a socialist; I wish they had recognized that fact from his rhetoric when he was running for president. Obama was be able to cause a lot of damage before he could no longer run for president and his democratic congress removed. It is true when we make bad decisions in life, most often we end up having to pay the piper and I'm afraid America will not escape unscathed from the Obama administration decisions.

President Trump has successfully removed many of the bad decisions but some still remain that are more difficult to cancel.

If you are still able to fool yourself into thinking our country has not been moving toward socialism, how about this fact; in 1950 28% of Americans received help in some form from Government programs, while today it's almost 50%.

Let's go back and look at the immigration mess. I would like to compare the illegal immigration of about 20 million mostly from Mexico and Central America; the latest estimates (yes I am racial profiling) to our relations with China.

In both cases, the drain on jobs and money in our economy is huge. The argument supporting the illegal workforce was the claim they were doing stoop labor in the farm fields that the farmers could not get American workers to perform; this may have been the case 3 or 4 decades ago but is no longer true.

While some are working the farms and are needed, illegal immigrants are now framing houses, painting, adding additions, working in meat processing plants and on and on. Are we saying that none of the unemployed or those that are underemployed would be willing to work at any of those jobs?

I will admit that I know a person that owns a nursery located in a very poor county in North Carolina. This county has almost no manufacturing or good paying jobs of any kind. You would think the people that live there would be thrilled to get a job at his nursery. He pays 10 dollars an hour for unskilled trade and this was in 2004. He couldn't find any locals to work so he hired Mexicans. He pointed out they were excellent workers. Is it also possible that our society has created lazy unreliable workers who expect much for doing little? Perhaps we have not had to live in the poverty of the average Mexican and therefore lack the drive and ambition to achieve a better life.

Perhaps part of the problem with the job market is twofold; the immigrants will work for less money and it's been reported they are more reliable and do better work. The average hourly compensation costs in Mexico is $6.48 while in the United States it's $35.53. If a Mexican worked for half the wage, it would still be almost three times what he would make in Mexico. It's easy to see why the companies like to hire illegal immigrants. Some immigrants pay taxes and some do not. Those not eligible for Social Security can apply for a tax identification number; there is no way to know how much the State and Federal governments lose in tax revenue each year.

It is estimated that the dollars sent back to Mexico in 2013 was 22 billion; this money is not going back into our economy. 22 billion dollars would provide 550,000 people with a $40,000 a year job.

President Thump realizes the illegal immigrant problem is even more than jobs and money although the amount spent giving illegals assistance is enormous; the drugs and crime make it even more important that we correct a broken system. Most drugs come across the border from Mexico with illegals and this should not surprise anyone since the drug cartels practically control Mexico.

How does the illegal immigrant situation compare with China?

Do you remember Presidential candidate Ross Perot running in 1992? Ross had many ideas that I personally could not accept from a president but he had two ideas that even at the time I felt were right on the money; stop outsourcing American jobs, and don't pass NAFTA. If you're not that familiar with NAFTA, it stands for North America Free Trade Agreement. This agreement between the United States, Canada, and Mexico effectively suspended tariffs on products. Tariffs were used to level the playing field for products coming into the United States. A product produced in Mexico where the worker's pay is about 15% of the American worker would be much cheaper so the tariff would keep the American product competitive.

President Trump being a businessman recognized this problem and has taken action to correct it; how could the Democrats and Republicans in past administrations not seen the same truth? Trump working with Mexico and Canada is in the process of renegotiating the defective treaty.

Once NAFTA was passed, American companies like the auto makers, could have parts made in Mexico and brought into the United States much cheaper than manufacturing them in our country; goodbye many manufacturing jobs in the United States and many dollars leave our economy.

Canada was not as big a problem since our economies are very similar but Mexico is more of a third world or I think it is more politically correct to refer to Mexico as a developing country, and our labor force can not possibly compete with their pitifully low wages. While Canada is not a big problem like China and Mexico, they still have practices that restrict our farmers from sending our goods to Canada.

China poses a serious problem for the United States since we have free trade with them. Their wages are even lower than Mexico and while they don't have illegal immigrants living here; almost everything we buy today is manufactured in China.

In 2013 China imported from the United States 122 billion in products and we imported from China 440 billion; that's a trade deficit of 318 billion dollars. Unlike the illegal immigrants from Mexico, China doesn't pay taxes or put anything into our economy.

When was the last time you purchased almost any product that didn't say "made in China". What has happened to so many of our manufacturing plants? We no longer have the capability to produce many of our goods.

The argument made by Bill Clinton and many others in support of the free trade agreements was that manufacturing jobs would be lost but replaced by higher paying jobs. I had to agree with Ross Perot that this would never happen. I tried to visualize the person on a manufacturing line that installed power cords on a toaster, retrained and is now a computer programmer. It's never going to happen. The politicians said we wouldn't have a big trade imbalance with china because they would buy things from us that they didn't make. The 318 billion for one year trade deficit proved them wrong. If you don't think China is the real beneficiary of free trade; how do you suppose they were able to loan the United States almost one trillion dollars that were needed to keep the country running?

Most of the clothing mills in North Carolina are no more. It would be interesting to know where those people are now working and even more interesting; how much they are paid compared to the jobs they lost.

An interesting observation concerning losing so much of our manufacturing capability is the fact that the Civil War most likely would have turned out differently had the South had the manufacturing capability of the North. The south had the best generals in Lee, Longstreet and forest and the southern soldiers were so dedicated toward the end of the war they were fighting barefoot with clubs. The South had to get its arms, ammunition and other manufactured goods from Europe and an effective blockade by the North crippled the South which was primarily engaged in agriculture.

I hope the situation never arises where we need more manufacturing capability in the future.

President Trump recently stated that loss of manufacturing was a security issue not just a jobs loss, when you look at the effect of low manufacturing capability during the Civil War, he is right on the money.

What I see happening is the American consumer is now able to purchase items they would not be able to afford if they were made in the United States. A few items I can think of to compare would be, a fancy birdbath that if manufactured locally might cost $200 can now be purchased for $50 or $60 dollars made in China. The average income earner that never could have spent $200 on a birdbath can now afford $60.

Fancy lighted outside Christmas decorations fall under the same category along with all the decorations; we can get a string of lights for a few dollars. These are only a couple of areas out of a multitude, and all of these represent lost American manufacturing jobs.

Now all of us being able to afford so many nice things that we could not have when they were "Made in the USA" would be all well and good, IF, China was as some predicted buying an equivalent amount of products or services from the United States so the people that lost the manufacturing jobs would still be employed and at similar pay. Again, the trade deficit with China shows that did not happen.

In 2009 the average manufacturing compensation in China in US dollars was $1.74 cents; now how many American products do you think the people in China are going to buy from the United States when making only $1.74? A happy meal at McDonalds cost between $3.00 and $4.00 so a days pay would let them buy about four happy meals for there kids.

It's not too difficult to understand why we have such a huge trade deficit with china.

Let's see how well the United States fared with free trade; our 2013 deficit with China was 318 billion, with Mexico 54 billion, with Canada

31 billion with all other countries, 308 billion for a 2013 grand total trade deficit of 680 billion. This money all went into supporting the economies of our foreign trading partners. Could this possibly have caused a loss of jobs?

Vice President Joe Biden said that there was no way to restore the eight million jobs lost during the recession and I believe he is right as long as the United States continues to send 680 billion a year to other countries to keep their people employed.

President Trump has proved the former Vice President wrong by discontinuing regulations that help kill manufacturing jobs and placing tariffs on other countries products that are putting our companies out of business, Tariffs were especially needed on products from China and Mexico due to their low standard of living and poor wages. Trump is also dealing with countries who restrict many of our products to protect their own while we allow their products in and compete with our manufacturers; if they don't restrict the import, they place a higher tariff to restrict their sales.

If that 680 billion a year we are sending to foreign countries were to stay in the United States, it would provide 17 million jobs at $40,000 a year.

The housing market is a classic example of the blind leading the blind. In the great depression people were defaulting on their home mortgages en masse resulting in a shortage of funds at the banks.

In 1938 Franklin Roosevelt and the congress created Fannie Mae to buy mortgages from lenders to free up capital. Banks now felt free to loan money to low and middle income borrowers that they previously might not have considered creditworthy. In 1968 it was converted into a publicly traded company owned by investors. In 1970 Freddie Mac was started mainly to prevent Fannie Mae from being a monopoly; in 1989 Freddie Mac also went pubic.

These two companies are the largest holders of mortgages in the country and President Jimmy Carter, President Bill Clinton and President George Bush all played important roles in the current housing debacle.

In 1977 the Carter administration and congress passed the Community Reinvestment Act which required banks that had FDIC insurance help meet the credit needs of the community in which they operated including low and moderate income neighborhoods. The act did not require that banks lower their standards for safe and sound business practices.

Now I'm not sure how a bank was supposed to accomplish giving a low income individual a good business practice sound judgment loan. The very concept of the government pressuring banks to make loans to low income people, smacks of socialism but we won't take away from the fact that officially, the act did not require banks to lower their low requirement standards: however, if the banks could loan money to low income people while practicing good judgment and sound business practices, why weren't they already doing it? The very fact that the person is low income indicates to any reasonable person, they would have a difficult time providing base essentials let alone handle a bank loan. The whole program sounds more like the government encouraging banks to take greater risk.

In 1999 the Clinton administration pressured Fannie Mae to expand loans to low and moderate income borrowers by taking on a higher percentage of these loans in distressed inner city areas.

The Democrats are still trying to make everyone equal which has never been or ever will exist in this world. Perhaps they have never read the statement in the bible by Jesus that said the poor will be with you always; I keep forgetting, they may not believe the bible; well it's been 2000 years and the poor are still with us in spite of the ever increasing massive government attempts to change that.

The banking system is now involved in the sub prime lending business, which means they are lending money to but houses, cars, credit cards etc. to people in the highest risk category. Does this appear to be good judgment and sound business practices?

In 2002 President George W Bush (the so called conservative) signed an act that would give 2.4 billion in tax credits over the next five years to investors and builders who develop affordable single family housing in distressed areas. Do you think the people that buy those houses are going to be the sub prime borrowers?

It's now 2003 and the Bush Administration, it appears, was starting to realize the housing finance industry is not being managed properly. Bush wanted a new agency under the treasury department to assume supervision of Fannie May. The new agency would set capital reserve requirements and determine if the company was managing the risks of its portfolios. How about that old saying (better late than never), could that apply here?

The Democrats didn't like the plan; Representative Barney Franks the ranking Democrat on the Financial Services Committee stated "these two entities Fannie Mae and Freddie Mac are not facing any kind of financial crises" Barney went on to say "the more people exaggerate these problems, the more pressure there is on these companies, the less we will see in affordable housing" affordable housing means low income high risk.

Talk about famous last words, the companies that Barney Franks said were not in trouble will require at least 160 billion to fix and the cost could reach (hang onto your hats and your socks) one trillion dollars. For those not into large figures, that's 1000 billion! Now Barney Franks only interest was in making sure the sub prime lending didn't dry up so the low income people that couldn't afford to make a mortgage payment could still get a loan. That makes a lot of sense doesn't it?

The far left just can't seem to help themselves; they want to make sure everyone in America owns a home even if they can't afford one. They are probably still working on a government plan to pay for their homes with money we don't have and can't afford; perhaps borrowed from China!

If you think the Republicans were much smarter than the Democrats, explain this; the Republicans controlled congress at that time and they failed to introduce legislation aimed at the President Bush's proposal becoming law.

Even if the Republican Congress had passed the Bush proposal, it would have been too late to avoid the housing market meltdown because sub prime lending had been going on unsupervised for too long a time; at the very best it would have reduced the impact.

If you think from my writing that I see most Democrats as irresponsible Socialists, totally lacking in common sense; you would have come to the proper conclusion; if on the other hand you think that I'm a dyed in the wool Republican supporter, you missed the mark by a long shot.

The old Republican Party (going back a few decades) was a fiscally conservative group that supported the free enterprise system. They didn't support a lot of welfare, instead expected a person to work hard to support themselves. There are always exceptions for people that need a helping hand due to unusual circumstances; but this should be exceptions, not the rule. I already pointed out that today half the people in the United States receive some form of assistance from government programs and these figures are absolutely ridiculous.

I have supported the Republican Party for many years but until a single financial donation was given some time ago, I withheld contributing to the party for in my eyes they had become the party of do nothing. I now have changed my registration to unaffiliated.

While I'm no longer registered as a republican; since Donald Trump became president, I have started supporting the party which I believe could achieve many great changes if they can hold the House in the midterm elections and elect a few more republican senators and replace those that did not support the Trump agenda. It's hard to believe the American voters would give control of the House of Representatives to the Democrats after all the good things that have occurred under the Trump administration; lowest unemployment in 50 years, largest wage increases in a decade, many manufacturing jobs returning that leading democrats said would never come back and under their policies were right.

It is unbelievable to me that the Bush Administration and a Congress controlled by the Republican Party accomplished almost nothing; what in the world happened to them? As far as George Bush is concerned I now, equate him with Dr Jekyll and Mr. Hyde and I say this because when I look at Bush in his first term and compare his actions or lack of, with his second term, the change is about equal, what happened to him?

Now there will be those in the Republican Party that will dispute my claim that the party accomplished almost nothing; but according to that old saying (the proof is in the pudding) my claim is supported by many

Americans; otherwise, an upstart, inexperienced radical like Obama would never have been elected.

I believe the change that many Americans were looking for was not the radical socialist changes of the Obama Administration but a change from doing nothing to doing something constructive; it looks like we have been shortchanged by both the Republicans and Democrats.

The change Americans were looking for popped up in the most unexpected place, a person who had never ran for political office at any level decided to run for president, Donald Trump. Now there were 16 well known political figures running as well, so who would have thought this person would stand any chance of being the nominee for the Republican Party; no more cool talk just lots of action.

Americans have heard a lot of talk over the years by politicians from both parties but in all fairness I have to award 1st prize to Obama; this man can talk the longest in response to a single question, of any president during my lifetime and end up saying absolutely nothing of substance.

I'm sure anyone who cooks has at some time seen a recipe in a magazine or other source that looked wonderful and the ingredients sounded great, and after you tried it, you gave it to the dog and the dog turned his nose up. The proof is in the pudding applies here because it doesn't make any difference how good a recipe looks or how much you like the ingredients; the results is all that count.

Obama can talk an Eskimo into buying a refrigerator and he knows it and loves to here himself talk, you can see this when he is being questioned; he goes on and on and on, and when he's done, your not sure what his answer was or if he answered it at all; but when you look at the results of his presidency; I'm sorry, but it makes you want to barf up that pudding.

I haven't seen that commercial for years put out by Star-Kist Tuna and if you're fairly young you have probably never seen it. The commercial had a tuna named Charlie who was always trying to get chosen by Star-Kist. In one commercial he was playing the piano and the response was "sorry Charlie, Star-Kist wants tuna that taste good, not tuna with good taste". Well President Obama, America wanted a president that does well not one that talks good.

CHAPTER 10

What's going to Happen America?

Depression?

Most likely one of the major concerns on the mind of most Americans today is; will the recession turn into a depression? It is my opinion that it will be a miracle if not only America, but the whole world is able to escape really tough times.

Perhaps if President Trump gets the support he needs; first from the people, then from the congress, he can turns things around; we'll see!

The really scary part is how this modern generation will be equipped to deal with hard

Times. The people that endured the great depression of the 1930's didn't have the easy life we have today; they worked hard and had very little in the way of things and services so there wasn't a whole lot for them to give up when the depression hit, but the most notable difference is in the attitudes and basic values of people today.

People today act like the good life is owed to them rather than being given the opportunity to work hard and earn what they get. This attitude is reflected in many aspects of their lives. This attitude was created when they were children and continues today.

Today children receive too much allowance and they are required to do nothing to earn it. The parents are so busy making money that they don't even know how their kids are spending the money. I think one of the reasons they are given so much money is Mom works and is not at home to do all the things that non working moms are able to, so they handle their guilt with money. The other scenario is divorced parents, which statistics show that 37% of children don't grow up with both biological parents. The children play the parents for money and gifts as they are aware the parents are competing for their love

After being showered with money and gifts while growing up, as I pointed out already, companies had to lower their expectations because that was the only kind of employees they would have to choose from(could it be that outsourcing is a way around this?)

The government continues the process with various programs; that keep young people from having to work hard and make sacrifices. The college loan programs are a perfect example; the students don't have to work, they just borrow the money. They are supposed to pay it back when they graduate and get a job, but as of 2009 the statistics show about 50 billion dollars in loan defaults. The nice thing from the students viewpoint is by not having to work weekends or nights, there is plenty of time for drinking and partying; after all isn't that what college is for; I mean of course the education to gain employment is a nice side effect Can you believe that the student loans now exceed the total credit card debt in America?

We now have our government shelling out vast sums of money to fund every kind of program know to man and even some they don't know about. How long can both the government and individual people keep spending borrowed money before the bottom drops out? I believe we will get that answer shortly.

At the G20 conference in Toronto Canada in June 2010, they were requesting that the deficit for the major countries involved be cut by 50% within 3 years; it ended up by allowing each country to make their own decision about the balance between debt recovery and recession recovery. It appears to me that when they ended up, they were right back where they started.

The problem for the United States can be summed up like this;

The government spends more money than it makes in taxes which results in having to borrow money to make up the shortfall or reduce government spending. (We know the government never really reduces spending)

The unemployment rate and underemployment was in double digits which means the government was taking in even less taxes; thus, more borrowing.

This has been corrected by President Trump. The unemployment rate in now 3.5% the lowest in 50 years. Depression loomed in the near future but now things are turning around.

The government under Obama borrowed more money, not to run the government programs but to provide a government stimulus that was to reduce unemployment.

Unemployment stayed the same but the government now has to pay additional interest on the debt pushing them further into the hole.

Obama administration had appointed a commission to come up with recommendations to restrict the national debt to 3% of the nation's economy by 2015 which means we would still be spending more that we bring in taxes by over 400 billion a year. The total debt would still be growing and the only method to borrow less than we are currently is to raise taxes or cut spending or both.

Any reduction in the yearly national debt will necessarily require that money be taken out of the economy. Less money flowing into the economy means higher unemployment. If this were not true, why would Obama borrow money from China for a stimulus to create jobs; or why did he not want to reduce the yearly budget deficit by 50% in 3 years because he was afraid it would have a negative effect on the economic recovery?

How about the 21 trillion we already owe for all the years of living beyond our means? The United States can't even begin to start paying down this debt until we can run our government without borrowing and then reach a point where we have money left over to pay on the 21 trillion. Keep in mind when this book gets published, the debt will be even larger since we still won't live within our means.

Did I talk about reducing the National Debt? The figures that came from the Obama Administration, is that when the total projected budget deficits are added to the current debt, the total debt will be way over 20 trillion dollars by 2020, WOW! It's 2018 and already past there.

The Republicans and some Democrats and independents knew the stimulus was not going to create jobs by the government handing out money. The only way to create jobs is to cut taxes so people will have more money to spend and business will be more prone to hiring.

President Trump has passed the largest tax cut in history and the economy has boomed and huge amount of jobs created but the cut in regulations also contributed to more jobs.

If you cut taxes the government will bring in less money and thus have to borrow more; the theory being that when the unemployed start going back to work, they will be paying taxes; also the government won't have to pay them unemployment. It's my understanding that's what happened with the Reagan tax cuts to turn around the Jimmy Carter recession. One not so pleasant fact is that the national debt almost tripled; so the government revenues increased with the tax cuts but the deficit increased; do you suppose our government started spending more?

The national debt in 1989 the last year of President Reagan equaled about half our nations GDP (gross domestic product); while in 2009 it had risen to 86% and now 100%. What this means is that it would require all the money that every American makes for a year to pay off the national debt.

From all that I see, the Clinton Administration did a very good job with the finances when compared to other presidents. Clinton increased the national debt by 1.1 trillion or 25% while the GDP increased by 3.2 trillion or 47%. We have to keep in mind the country was in pretty good shape when he became president.

Looking at the Reagan presidency will find totally different results because Reagan inherited a miserable economy from Jimmy Carter; unemployment was at 7.7% and the inflation rate at an unbelievable rate of 12%. Interest and loan rates were at 14 % to 16 %. Reagan increased the national debt by 1.5 trillion or 161% while the GDP increased by 2 trillion or 67%.

After the Clinton Presidency it was all down hill.

The last year of Ronald Reagan's presidency the National Debt was 2 trillion 684 billion.

The last year of Bush senior's presidency the National Debt was 4 trillion 177 billion.

The last year of Bill Clinton's presidency the National Debt was 5 trillion 662 billion.

The last year of George Bush's presidency the National Debt was 10 trillion 699 billion.

The last year of Barack Obama's Presidency the National Debt was 19.9 trillion

George Bush increased the National Debt in his eight years as President by 5 trillion 37 billion which was 661 billion less than all three presidents preceding him that served a total of twenty years.

George Bush cut taxes but not spending which added huge amounts to the National Debt and the interest we have to pay on that debt.

Obama despite the start of a recession, added new government programs and ended his terms increasing the National Debt by over 9 trillion.

There are three major reasons I find it hard to believe America can avoid really hard times and they are:

Social Security
Medicare
Medicaid

The amount of money the Federal Budget will require over the coming years to fund these three programs is staggering!

I won't discuss Medicaid because it is a welfare program and the people that benefit from this program have never paid a single dime to qualify for its benefits.

Social Security and Medicare on the other hand, people have been paying into for all the years they worked or will work. Earlier I showed how much money Social Security and Medicare recipients would have if the government would have let them invest the money. Today they wouldn't have to worry if the government could keep sending their checks or paying for their medical.

Even if the government didn't let them invest their own money but had invested all of their payments from Social Security and Medicare, the programs would be self sufficient today; but the government robbed the programs and made it a pay as you go program.

What that means to those of you that are still working is as more and more Baby Boomers qualify for these benefits, the government will have no choice but to raise the percentage taken out of your paycheck. If they don't raise the money that way they will have to raise your income tax or disallow certain deductions; and there is always new taxes. How they raise your taxes is not important only that they do.

The bottom line is this; the Federal Government owes 21 trillion dollars in debt and it doesn't bring in enough taxes to pay the day to day running of the government; couple this with huge increased needs for Social Security and Medicare, what is going to happen?

We might as well talk about the troops in Iraq and Afghanistan because the cost of these wars when added to all of our other financial fiascos just adds fuel to the fire. The total cost of these two wars from 2003 thru 2010 is approximately one trillion dollars.

I have been supportive of the Bush Administration attempt to establish Democracies in these countries in the hope of stopping the terrorist groups from controlling the countries. This plan was probably the only hope of settling that part of the world; even if it was a slim hope; but I'm starting to reassess the entire situation.

The argument that establishing Democracies would stabilize the region is certainly believable; what's not believable to me is that it is possible to attain. I no longer believe the Arab world will ever operate like the United States and Europe. These cultures have been around for thousands of years since early biblical times and have never on their own created a democratic form of government; why do we think we can change that by any means? I am aware that Iraq had elections but that is a long way from establishing a Democracy and once we totally leave the country, we currently have about 5000 troops mainly acting as advisers, wonder how long it will survive.

Is oil a factor in the United States involvement in the Middle East? I don't see how any industrialized Nation in the World could possibly afford to ignore the catastrophic results if terrorist groups gained control of oil resources in the Middle East. If all oil from OPEC were to stop, the economies of all industrialized Nations would collapse. The real truth is, if that were to happen, the West would have no choice but to take over the oil wells by force if necessary; so is oil a concern; you bet.

President Trump is opening up more areas in the United States for oil exploration that Obama had shut down and we are now the largest producer of oil and natural gas in the world. If we keep going we can become independent of oil from the Middle East but Europe will not.

I've just made a case for the United States not to be dependent on foreign oil, and wouldn't it be wonderful? How do you suppose we are to accomplish such a feat? If you listen to those that say green energy is the answer, I would have to say that I don't believe it's even remotely possible. Let's look at some facts!

Let's start with automobiles. There are about 250 million automobiles in the United States. Are we saying we're going to replace these with electric cars or hybrids? Do you think the people could scrap all these cars and afford to buy even more expensive ones? Maybe they could pay to convert their cars to electric or hybrid. If the American people had that kind of money, which we know they don't, how many decades would it take to produce or convert that many cars? Some of these cars are now being sold but in tiny numbers as there are many problems to resolve.

They have limited range and you can't take a trip because there are not any charging stations. Charging may take over night which would require lodging while you wait. There are ideas such as battery swapping stations that are being considered but all such plans are way off in the future. Since we are converting from gasoline to electricity, won't this require expanding all of the power plants in the United States to handle the increased load? What kind of energy do the power plants use; oil, coal?

Now let's add the current population growth in the United States is .77 percent per year which means we will add about 2.5 million to our population this year and they will need cars and most will use gasoline.

While about 70 percent of our oil use is for transportation, the next biggest use of oil is for power plants. To eliminate the use of oil the plants would have to convert to coal or nuclear. Coal is not considered green energy so there would be a problem switching to coal from oil.

Nuclear energy for our power plants is the only viable green energy source. At this time the United States gets about 19 percent of its energy from nuclear power. Converting the other 82% to nuclear will take decades. The average length of time from start to finish for a nuclear power plant is 10years.

What about solar and wind power, they're green and the energy source is free? There may be limited applications for these but I don't see in the foreseeable future reducing much need on oil because of the sun or wind. Both of these sources of energy require backup power generation. The wind doesn't blow all the time and there are only a few states where they would be practical at all; the same is true for the sun, cloudy days and nighttime. The cost of having dual methods for producing power would be very expensive. How many solar cells would it take to power New York City and how many acres of land?

Realistically, we are going to require a lot of oil for decades no matter what anyone tells you. The environmentalist are so concerned about the planet that they fool themselves into believing we can operate our cars and power our homes all on green power. None of us alive today will live to see that happen.

Let's look at Obama's Cap and Trade bill which would place a tax on emissions that is estimated to cost the taxpayers about 200 billion a year. Now the claim by the Democrats is that we need to do this to save the environment or reduce Global Warming but we now know that the figures released that made claims about Global Warming were exaggerated, distorted and facts that disputed their claims were covered up. The facts were so misrepresented that people were demanding that Al Gore return the Nobel Prize he received jointly with the UN's Intergovernmental Panel on Climate Change. There have also been requests that Al Gore return the academy award for the movie Inconvenient Truth.

It was hackers that obtained EMAILS from The University of East Anglia's Climate Research Unit organization that showed their claims were perpetrated by fraud. The Climate Research Unit provides the data to the UN's panel on climate change. Scientists at the unit distorted the research to cover up the fact that for the last 10 years the Global Climate has actually been cooling.

Climate change is no doubt a fact because the climate is constantly changing; Thanksgiving day in Raleigh North Carolina this year, the high temperature was 50 degrees while the highest temperature on this day was 80 degrees in 1900; the historical average is 61 degrees. Was that 19 degree above average temperature a sigh of global warming or climate change? Could it possibly been caused by man? There were 76,000,000 people living in the United States and they owned a total of 8000 automobiles.

I will say again, if you don't want to be the blind following the blind, pay attention to who you are getting your facts from. Even if you thought the scientists at the Climate Research Center wouldn't have a personal agenda that would permit them to distort the truth; you now know it's dangerous to ever assume you have the facts. If an organization's records are not open to scrutiny at all times, be very skeptical of anything they claim.

Scientists are now looking at Mars since the probe landed there to try and determine the origin of the universe; I wonder if this will turn out like their determining that man probably started as I single cell washing up out of the ocean and after millions of years evolved into man. Scientists now have determined that persons DNA is so complex that it could not have occurred by accident but required intelligent design; isn't it great to have science to reaffirm what the bible for thousands of years already told us. God created man and that is the intelligent design. After spending billions of dollars that could go to much better projects, is science going to tell us after extensive exploration we have determined that the universe was created by intelligent design? Will we say to them, God created the universe on day four and we have known about it for thousands of years.

So now that we know that there is no valid proof that any change in climate has any bearing on fossil fuels; why was the Obama Administration still pushing for the Cap and Trade legislation? Is it possible that Cap and Trade is a really a sneaky way to increase taxes under the guise of saving the earth? Would politicians really do something like that? A recent poll finds that 73 percent of the people don't trust the politicians in Washington; maybe the other 27 percent didn't understand the question.

Cap and Trade as currently written was defeated this is a victory for all of us. Taking another 200 billion out of the economy in the form of energy taxes could only make things worse and I am glad there were enough members of congress both Democrats and Republicans that recognized this, to stop this bill in its tracks.

So the big question that everyone is mulling over; will we have a depression, just can't be answered for sure. I believe if it's not right away; it can't be far down the road. It's hard for me to believe that our government policies since the great depression were in any way developed using common sense and responsible judgment.

President Trump is trying to turn the country around and has accomplished much, but after many decades of irresponsible decisions; is it going to be enough? Only time will tell.

While we are encouraged by the government to save for our retirement and for any rainy days that crop up from time to time during a person's lifetime, the government didn't practice what it preached; I guess they like the more modern saying(don't do as I do, do as I say). Our government didn't put anything away for recessions or wars or any other unexpected needs such as natural disasters; they just robbed the entitlement programs and when that was gone, borrowed, borrowed, and borrowed some more.

Since the government already plans to keep borrowing hundreds of billions each year for many years to come, maybe they hope to stave off the depression until our debt is so huge that no one will loan us any more; of course why worry about that because it would happen on someone else's watch. The down side to that thinking is it wouldn't prevent the sitting president at that time from placing the blame on the previous president or presidents; we have certainly seen enough of this from Obama.

The Democrat Party has certainly changed over the years; what happened to the well known standard by former President Harry Truman who he had on a sign on his desk (The Buck Stops Here). Harry Truman assumed final responsibility as President of the United States. He was a very humble man who once made the statement "three things can ruin a man, power, money, and women, I never wanted power, I never had any money, and the only woman in my life is up at the house right now".

Harry Truman had only been Vice President for less than a year when Roosevelt died. He had to handle the end of World War two which included the toughest decision a president could have to make; dropping two atomic bombs to save the lives of an estimated one to two million Americans and more than a million Japanese civilians. Truman had to handle the Korean War as well.

America needed a President today much like Harry Truman; a man who is decisive and takes responsibility for his decisions; does this sound like a description of President Trump?

Let's see what the election in 2018 brings us. Will the majority of American voters be so blind that they will return the left wing socialists back to power? God forbid!

Terrorism

Terrorism has to be a real concern for all Americans and I believe that most all experts in this area will agree that the question is not if, but when and where the next terrorist attack will take place.

There is probably no country on earth that has more emphasis on terrorist than Israel; this country is surrounded by Muslims that hate them so they have no choice but to take major steps to protect their people. Even with all of their precautions, Israel still has people killed, so how can we expect the United States to fare better?

We have a no fly list in an attempt to keep terrorists out of the country and we've already seen how it has failed. There are going to be Muslims that are not on the list that make it into the country. Flying is not the only way into the United States, our border with Mexico doesn't just allow illegal immigrants who want to work to gain access. If millions of workers, drug dealers etc have crossed the border over the years, do you suppose some terrorists may also have entered the United States the same way?

For all the faults of the Bush Administration, security was not one of them and he needs to be given credit for enacting policies that have been keeping us safe. One of those policies that came under attack from the far left was being able to monitor calls from Muslims in the Middle East to Muslims in American without going to a judge and request a warrant. The concern of the far left was privacy rights (big brother is watching) which in my opinion were totally ridiculous as long as they are monitoring Muslims, in other words profiling, since they are the source of terrorism. Can you believe the same Democrats that disagreed have now been caught monitoring every American and half of Europe's leaders; talk about hypocrisy!

The Democrats wanted a requirement that in order to monitor Muslims you would have to go through a judge and that is exactly what they did when they wanted to monitor American citizens, the Pfizer court. So did that work to prevent them from illegal monitoring?

They presented false unverified reports to the court implying the information had been vetted when it had not. As a result we are still in an investigation of President Trump based on that false information that has created a terrible mess and cost the American tax payers millions. All of this was done to attack President Trump because they hated his ideas and he defeated their darling Hillary Clinton who has shown she has a hard time always the truth. I laughed when she was being interviewed on a left leaning network and was asked" do you always tell the truth" and her response was "I always try to", well that's nice but the next question which didn't come should have been; are you always successful. It's not what you try it's if your successful.

A final note on Bush; his one failing on security was not securing the borders. Not one president can take credit for making even a minimal attempt to stop people from crossing from Mexico into the United States. Bush, Clinton and Obama all publicly stated it was imperative that the border be secured but none of them did one thing to make it happen.

President Trump on the other hand is working hard to get a wall built with little help from the republicans and absolutely no help from the Democrats who want open borders.

The Obama Administration thought by talking sweetly to the radical Muslims, they will view us in a different light; they may be right;

the Muslims have viewed America as corrupt, immoral, imperialistic, infidels; now they have added weak to their evaluation. Obama is unbelievably naïve for a man of his age; he appears to think that Islam and the Christian religion are similar to the difference between Christianity and Buddhists, or Hindus, or even the differences between Christian Denominations. He can't seem to accept the fact that the Muslim religion is a very violent religion in spite of their constant rhetoric about a peaceful religion. If you don't accept the Muslim religion, you are considered by most to be an infidel and they have no love for you.

The Bush Administration ran into a problem in Afghanistan when the followers of Islam demanded of the leader in the country, Karzai, to execute a man who some 14 years before had converted to Christianity; the man's own father agreed he should be executed; converting to Christianity is considered an intolerable insult. It was quite a situation for an American President who has provided troops and money in an attempt to create a democracy. The end result was that Karzai arranged to have him deported which helped to diffuse a volatile religious conflict.

I'm really going to start a firestorm with this next analogy; in the end days when Christ returns to earth to rule with an iron hand(no more mister nice guy) there will be the great battle of Armageddon. In the 1980's I taught a College and Career Class at my Baptist Church; these were young people ages 19 to 35. During our discussion of Armageddon, many thought the USSR would be the army from the North mentioned in the bible, but I never believed the great battle would be country against country, but religious ideology against religious ideology.

It is my belief that it is not only very possible, but very likely; the final battle will be the Muslims against the Christians and Jews. The Muslim religion is legalistic and violent

With the goal to convert the entire world to their religion and by any means necessary.

It is the only religion that has its followers murdering thousands who don't accept the Muslim religion but even kill their own because of differences in their religious practices. Shite and Sunnis kill each other; therefore, if the final battle is religious, it will have to be with the Muslims.

We certainly have enough proof when you look at 2011 and all the bombings that take place killing men, women, and children on a regular basis and all committed by Muslims.

The Muslims generally hate the Jews and this is quite a mind boggler because their beliefs have much in common. Both religions believe in the God of Abraham and Moses, while they both believe Jesus was a prophet but not the Son of God.

In 2010, Muammar Gaddafi the former head of the African Country of Libya was attending the United Nations sponsored Global Food Summit in Rome Italy where he invited 200 women to a party where he presented them with a copy of the Koran and said "Convert to Islam, Jesus was sent for the Jews, not for you, Mohammed on the other hand, was sent for all human beings" He followed up with "Whoever goes in a different direction than Mohammed is wrong. God's religion is Islam, and whoever follows a different one, in the end, will lose"

Gaddafi's statement that Jesus came for the Jews is totally incorrect; he came to offer salvation to every single human being that was willing to follow him and that includes Muslims that convert. Keep in mind that Jesus had been resurrected 600 years before Muhammad came on the scene and the Arab world rejected him just as the Jews did.

Gaddafi in 2006 stated, in a few decades, the Muslims will take over Europe; there are now 50 million Muslins in Europe and he said when Turkey enters the European Union, there will be another 50 million Muslims. "Europe is in a predicament and so is America, they should agree to become Islamic in the course of time, or else declare war on the Muslims".

Unemployment

The unemployment problem had to be more than a bit scary. It's not just the number that were unemployed, it looked like it would get worse tomorrow? There are three things occurring that could cause even more American workers to lose their jobs; more Mexicans crossing the border, more jobs being outsourced to other countries, and more companies bringing in foreign workers especially in the high tech industries.

President Trump has been addressing unemployment by bringing back jobs that were sent Oversees, reducing unnecessary regulations and reducing corporates taxes and the result is reducing an unemployment and under employment rate of 10% to a 50 year low of 3.5%.

Over 23 million Americans were unemployed or under employed and the Obama Administration kept borrowing money from foreign countries to keep extending unemployment benefits with the hope times will get better and they will get jobs. The times were not getting better and the unemployed were still not getting jobs. When the Census Bureau hired some 700,000 census workers for temporary work, the unemployment rate dropped a few tenths of a percent. This time the Census Bureau hired way too many workers and many were being paid to do little work. The Census Bureau responded by saying they normally hire more than needed because many workers find better jobs and they would be left short; this was not the case this time because there were few job opportunities out there; surprise, surprise; you would think that should have been obvious to the casual observer since the unemployment rate at that time was almost 10%. Some critics had accused the Obama Administration of over hiring to lower the unemployment rate.

One thing you should keep in mind when looking at the unemployment figures released each month by the Government is the fact they do not represent a true figure of the unemployed; if people quit looking for work they are no longer considered unemployed so the unemployment rate appears to improve when it has not. The truth is the total number of Americans in the work force had gone down so perhaps instead of releasing unemployment figures each month, they should release employed figures to see if we are employing more people each month.

Isn't it interesting that President Thump when stating the unemployment rate was at a 50 year low of 3.5% also noted the number of employed Americans was the highest in history.

Everything our Federal and State Governments have done going back several decades, has contributed to our rising unemployment figures.

As I already discussed, parents and educators have created American workers that are under educated with a poor work ethic; therefore, many companies prefer foreign workers.

Even if the American worker was as reliable and capable as their foreign counterparts, it would be hard to compete for a job that the foreign workers will work at for much less.

This will always be the case when we allow workers from third world (I'm sorry, to be politically correct, I should say developing nations) to compete.

From the employer's perspective, if he can lower his salary costs enough; he may be more capable of competing with goods from China, Mexico, and others. At the very least he can improve the bottom line for his investors: speaking of investors, with the economy in such bad shape you wonder why the stock market was so high especially since total revenue is lower and the fact is total profits are up because they lowered costs by laying off employees.

Of course the stock market was nowhere near what it is under President Trump and peoples 401K, IRA or TDSP has grown significantly.

Job losses in the high tech industry can also be identified with the foreign workers being more desirable than comparable American workers. Everything that has taken place in our education system has resulted in students that graduate who can't read, write or do simple math. I don't know what we can do to fix that problem for those that have already graduated.

Outsourcing of jobs to Mexico, China, India, Taiwan, etc. because of cheap labor has cost Millions to lose their jobs. There is no way an American worker can compete with workers in a country where their pay is 10% to 15% of an American worker.

The estimated (no one knows for sure, not even your hairdresser) 12 to 15 million illegal workers (the latest estimates put it at over 20 million) are taking jobs that the unemployed could be working at; as I already pointed out, these jobs are not all involved in agriculture; many are in services and the building trades. I have no problem with farm laborers with a work permit but many of the other jobs can be filled by Americans; if they can't, then issue green cards to the immigrants; but first do a background check, get their picture, DNA sample and fingerprints.

Spending creates jobs, and I'm talking about individual not government spending. How will most Americans increase their spending without going deeper in debt just like the government? We already see that most Americans don't have any savings and aren't putting any back. In these uncertain times, no one wants to increase spending of borrowed money.

If the Bush tax cuts were allowed to expire, average taxpayers would be paying in the range of $500 to $2000 more a year in taxes which means they would have to reduce their spending by that much; goodbye to more jobs. The Obama administration only wanted to let the tax cuts for those making over $200,000 to expire but since only 4% make that much, how much help would that be; it's a drop in a very large bucket. President Obama himself admitted it wouldn't fix anything, so why was he wasting time on this issue if it won't help? He claims he only wanted to be fair but it sounds more like an attempt to cause resentment and jealousy directed toward the wealthy. My concept of fair is the same tax rate for everyone so a person that makes twice as much pays twice as much in taxes, a flat tax is fair while a progressive one targets those better off.

Moral Decline

To those of us that believe the bible and read about the history of the Jews, we have to believe moral decline will result in more devastation of the American way of life than, depression, terrorism and unemployment combined. In the Bible, God was never concerned over a person's finances, only how we live our lives.

There are two ways a nation loses when it enters a state of moral decline; God no longer assists the nation with its problems so life starts to deteriorate naturally; the second, no matter what anyone claims, God will bring disasters to that nation.

The liberal churches will claim that God is love and he doesn't cause disasters to happen; they must not be reading the same bible that I do.

Let's start with Sodom and Gomorrah; God sent three angels to see if the sins of those people were as bad as they thought; the end result being that God sent fire from heaven and totally destroyed all the people except Lot and his family.

When Moses came down from the mountain with the Ten Commandments, the people were conducting themselves immorally and were given the choice to follow God's laws or the world and its sin. For those that rejected God, about three thousand men were slain with the sword. God originally was going to destroy all of them but Moses pleaded for their sake and the Lord changed his mind.

On a more personal note, in the New Testament, there was the case of Ananias and his wife Sapphria. The people were selling land to raise money to support the needs of the Apostles. Ananias and Sapphria also sold land but held back part of the proceeds while claiming to have given the entire amount.

Peter said to Ananias, "why has Satan filled your heart to lie to the Holy Spirit", the land was his to keep or to sell but he wanted to get credit for giving the entire amount. Peter told Ananias "you have not lied to men, but to God"; when he heard these words, he dropped dead.

About three hours later Sapphria came in not knowing what had happened to her husband Ananias when Peter asks her "tell me whether you sold the land for such and such a price" and she said yes that was the price. Then Peter said to her "why is it that you have agreed together to put the Spirit of the Lord to the test" Behold, the feet of those who have buried your husband are at the door, and they shall carry you out as well" and she fell immediately at his feet and breathed her last.

While God is certainly filled with love for his creation, it would be foolish to ignore the reality that God gets fed up with our sinful nature and will respond accordingly. The great flood during Noah's day was the result of God seeing that the heart of man was constantly filled with wickedness.

If on the other hand, you don't believe in the bible or even in God, all of this is just fairytales and there is nothing to worry about. America can live anyway it chooses and if anything does happen, it will just be coincidence.

What exactly is wrong with America's morals? Keep in mind if you don't believe in God or the bible as his word, then there's no problem with any conduct as long as society will accept it, so I'm answering the question as a Christian.

Let's start with sex. The bible is very specific; sex is only ok between a man and a woman that are married.

Illicit sex is so rampant that some grade schools are issuing condoms and they don't require the parent's permission. This is in grade school, children 6 to 12 years old. When we move up to high school, many parents not only know their student is having sex but let them have sex in their own home. Their only concern is that the girl doesn't get pregnant as this would really mess up their education plans. The other concern is safe sex over their worry about sexually transmitted diseases. The moral implications have vanished because society pretty well accepts this conduct. Man is more concerned with how society views things than how God does even though God holds their very soul in his hands.

Hollywood, which includes movies and television have not only made it perfectly normal to sleep around but glamorize the practice. In almost every TV show or movie the main characters talk about or have sex with people they just met at the bar or similar place; basically one night stands. No one in these shows ever seems to have any guilt or remorse or shame; it's like enjoying a good meal; no more, no less.

With the entertainment industry outright endorsing free sex, there is one thing you almost never see in these shows; the people dying with AIDS and what their life styles are like during that slow death. There are 50,000 new cases of HIV each year in the United States and 15,000 die; yet the people continue their evil ways.

It's not just AIDS and other sexually transmitted diseases that results from the free sex attitude; both men and women no longer view each other with respect; the women are liberated and the men are glad because the women start sharing the costs and they don't have to marry them. The men and women become bitter and the relationship that God intended to exist between a man and a woman has disintegrated. You would think they would recognize what has happened and change; it only seems to get worse.

Look at the number of accusations of sexual assault, and grouping that are in the news almost daily, not many years ago you almost never heard of this; now some women would say, that's because we let the men get away with it for years. Now I don't approve of such conduct but women handled the problem themselves while now they are so against men they create huge problems and as I just said "the men and women become bitter".

Another big sell job by Hollywood is homosexuality. One reason Hollywood wants to convince main stream America that this practice is not a sin but merely a different lifestyle, is because so many in Hollywood are practicing homosexuals and lesbians. If Hollywood gets average Americans to accept this perverted conduct; they will be more comfortable being out in the open. Maybe the reason it's becoming easier to sell this type of conduct is because so many Americans are also living in sin, so if I accept your sin, you can accept mine; another old saying(you scratch my back and I'll scratch yours?)

It's reported that 52 percent of new HIV infections are from men having sex with men but because of bisexual activity and drug needle use, 31% are among heterosexuals. Of the 56,000 new HIV infections each year; more than 200,000 are not aware they are infected.

I've read the many theories about the origin of AIDS and no one knows for sure, but there is one fact that is the most important; if you don't have sex until your married and the same is true for your partner, and you don't commit adultery or enter into homosexual activity; you won't get AIDS. This lifestyle is exactly the way God instructed us to live. Do you suppose the origin of AIDS is God?

We know that men with men sex is the real source of the problem and heterosexuals contact it from needles or those that are bisexual in their practices. The bible which is the word of God condemns homosexuality; the bible says such conduct is an abomination in the eyes of God.

I believe that an even greater abomination is that people that don't practice homosexuality are becoming more and more willing to accept conduct that is offensive to our creator.

We know that going all the way back thousands of years to Sodom and Gomorrah there were homosexuals, yet AIDS didn't really appear until the early 1980's. I believe the reason God didn't create the AIDS virus until modern times is because it's purpose was to get the attention of those of us that began accepting what God considers perverted conduct; better known as sin!

The fate of the homosexual that will not repent and turn from his ways is already set with God so there's little point to addressing that problem; it's sort of like the fact that Jesus only mentioned the Sadducees one time in his ministry and only then when they challenged him about life after death. The Sadducees didn't believe in salvation because they didn't believe in eternal life; therefore, Jesus didn't waste his time on them. Jesus was always critical of the Pharisees but I believe because there was hope they might see the light and change their ways.

While I was still working, I had a young black man in his thirties come up to me one day asking if I had seen that report from the scientists that they expected to have a vaccine and cure for AIDS in two years. I told him I had seen the news and ask why he was so happy to hear this; of course, I had a pretty good idea. He informed me that it would be wonderful not to have to worry when dating.

I went on to tell this young man that I believed the Scientists were mistaken and that they would not have a cure in two years and not even in ten years. I did explain that I was not in any way knowledgeable of the virus from a medical or scientific perspective and my statement I believe is coming from God. I explained that I felt that God was using the AIDS virus to get our attention in a big way to convince us not to be supportive of sin and those that practice sin.

I'm not sure which year this conversation took place but I retired in 1996 so I'm guessing it was at least 22 years ago, and no vaccine or cure.

When discussing morals, how can we not talk about marriage; or should we say the lack of it? Not only do people have sex in one night stands, but when they hook up with someone they like, instead of getting married, they just live together; then have children out of wedlock. Often times those that lived together and had children never get married and the poor children end up in single parent homes. A single mother can not meet the needs of her children and neither can a single father. The people that live like this are being totally selfish and are showing no concern for the welfare of their child or they are so arrogant that they believe they are capable of being both father and mother.

Besides not being able to meet the needs of their children, they are now by example, teaching them that it is ok to live with someone and not get married so the problem just keeps expanding.

It was a rare occasion in the 1950's to see a couple living together and the reason was that they were either a Christian or society would have condemned their conduct and they would have been outcasts.

Has acceptance of ungodly conduct by parents and society as a whole helped move our people away from a relationship with God, or did the people living in the 1950's only live a more Godly life because they desired acceptance by their fellow man? I'm not sure anyone can really answer that question, for only God knows the heart of man; but one thing I do know; whatever their reason, the results were good.

One thing we need to understand, rules of conduct and laws are for the purpose of providing a society that can function and provide a decent place to live and raise children; it does not make people moral or godly; it merely forces them to conduct their lives in a manner that does not offend or place other members at risk.

CHAPTER 11

What can we do?

You know how I love to quote old sayings like "a stitch in time saves nine"; the moral to this saying is; fix it as soon as you see a problem; otherwise, it will require a lot of extra effort. I'm afraid we are way past the stitch in time so we are going to have to do the nine. Isn't it interesting that 9 years is how long the great depression lasted; or maybe not!

It's going to be a long slow haul to restore our country to any semblance of greatness and require great sacrifices. No one wants to face difficult times but if we don't get started right away it will only get more difficult.

Thumps theme when running for President was "make America great again" and he has already done much to improve our country economically; more than any president during my lifetime and when I was born Franklin Roosevelt was President so you can figure how many Presidents I have lived under.

Financial-Personal

Let's start with our financial dilemma; there are two areas we all have to address and we don't have to be an economists or financial wizard; government spending habits, and our own.

We might as well face the fact that in order to restore our country to fiscal responsibility. A protracted period of difficult times must be endured. Our own personal financial recovery and the State and Federal government's recovery can't really be separated because the governments have only one source of income to cover both their spending and their debt, and that's you and me; in fact, I shouldn't have said "their debt" because it's our debt.

Every penny spent by local, State, and Federal governments comes out of the individual taxpayer's income. The more the governments spend and borrow, the more they take from our income and the less we have left to deal with our own financial problems.

Some would say the businesses and corporations pay part of the tax but the truth is they include those taxes in the cost of their products and you and I still end up paying the tax. If the government didn't tax the business community, they could sell their products for less and we would have more money left to work on our personal debt.

The Obama Administration was in a quandary over the Bush tax cuts. Most economists wanted the tax cuts to remain; allowing them to expire would take billions out of the pockets of the American taxpayer and the result would be a loss of jobs. The government on the other hand would like to reduce the deficit spending in 2014 and beyond and this additional revenue would certainly help.

I see two problems with increasing individual taxes in the hopes of helping the budget deficit; more jobs lost means less taxes from those individuals and you have to pay them unemployment benefits; this looks like a lose, lose situation.

The other question is; if the tax cuts had expired and the government received more tax money, would they really apply it toward the budget deficit, or would they do what they always have in the past and spend it on new programs.

Changing our elected officials thinking about adding new programs and spend, spend, spend won't happen without real involvement by the people; we'll talk about that later.

Since it's easier to change our own way of thinking, let's start with us.

We have to start living within our means, and that doesn't mean owing our soul to the company store (in this case, the banks). We need to get back to the mindset of the 1950's where about the only thing a person bought on credit was a house or car. They saved up money each week from their paycheck to buy most everything else. That money in the bank also acted as an emergency fund and if an emergency did occur, you had to postpone that new purchase you were saving for.

We need one credit card and use it only for an emergency such as car trouble on the road and pay it off using our emergency fund. The credit card only acts as a convenient means of paying for the repair and not to convert to monthly payments.

Living within our means at this stage in the American lifestyle will require massive changes that no one will be very happy to implement, but if we don't, the result will be more difficult to bear than these changes.

By paying as you go it will mean for some not taking that cruise or vacationing at home; for others stop eating out except on special occasions. If these are not your weakness, you may have to cancel those expensive cell phone features and purchase the least expensive option.

Maybe you go out to movies regularly and buy those expensive treats or you rent movies from your cable or satellite provider. Those video games that you buy or rent for the kids may have to go, a great bonus would be if the kids had to go outside and ride bikes or skate or play ball or any of those healthy exercises that could end up causing them to lose the excess body fat which is a growing health concern.

How much do you give your kids every month? If they want spending money (I know this may be shocking to your children) how about mowing lawns or baby sitting; maybe even a part time job for the older ones.

There are dozens of ways that Americans blow their money and I've only mentioned a few. Each person needs to log every penny spent for several months and then set down and determine what could be eliminated or reduced. If you carry a credit card debt, the money you save should be applied to that debt until they are paid off. Once there paid off, don't start charging again.

Now there is a reality to reducing our personal spending to pay off our debt and save for retirement and rainy day emergencies; jobs will be lost! I can't think of any other way to get out of the hole we have dug for ourselves. We should have been doing this many years ago and if we had, the pain would be so much less; but we didn't! Here comes another old saying "don't cry over spilt milk"; the moral to this saying is, what's the point, what's done is done; pick up and move on.

You know, your teenager could actually survive without a car. The cost of purchasing the car and the yearly insurance, gas, maintenance etc. is huge; this savings alone would go a long way to achieving your goal of credit card debt free and money in the bank. You read this and say, oh no, my teenagers have to have a car; if they don't have a job, they don't need a car and a wonderful benefit is how many of the 2700 teens in 2010 died in wrecks or the 282,000 that are seriously injured would be prevented.

The previous figures are a bonus on top of the financial savings. Saving all that gas would also help make us energy independent.

We have become a throw away society and this not only adds to our cost of living but creates problems for land fills. It's hard to believe but Americans throw away 60 million plastic bottles a day. Let's compare this with the 1950's when only glass bottles were in use; Regular size soft drinks required a 2 cent bottle deposit and quart size a nickel. The bottles were returned to the grocery store for a refund; the bottles were picked up, washed and reused. If we were to go back to glass bottles and put a 25 cent deposit on them, we could save money and help the environment.

The bottles are just one of many items we throw away from razors to contact lenses I am amazed at how as Americans we squander our money; it's no wonder we are deep in debt and have little or no savings.

Paying more for bottled drinking water than for gasoline is hard to understand and we complain when gas prices go up by a few cents.

Car pooling would save a ton of money. In the 1950's my father car pooled with three other coworkers; each would drive for a week which saved each one 75 percent on their gasoline, tires, oil changes and mileage on their cars. When you think about that, if you drive 10,000 miles a year to work and back; that would be reduced to 2500 miles and the savings would be significant. With all that reduction in gasoline usage, think how much less money Americans would be sending to other countries. Think how much this could help our own economy to recover.

I've only mentioned a few ways we can start to get our own finances in order; I'm sure if each of us looked at our own spending habits, we could come up with many more.

I want to repeat myself here and say the changes needed are huge and it is difficult for people to make such drastic changes, but I would remind you that was exactly what Americans had to do after the stock market crash in 1929 and the subsequent depression. Perhaps if Americans today will start making the changes voluntarily right now; we won't have to go through such a long period of sacrifice and suffering.

We will move on to the problem of government spending after I leave you with this thought; If you lost your job as 25% of Americans did in the great depression; what would happen to your home, your car, or your children's education?

Financial - Government

Our government's policies and spending habits have to be devastating to the American economy. Since most Americans are spending almost everything they make and then borrowing more; how could it be that unemployment was so high?

If the money we spent was staying in the United States economy under Obama, and add to that all of the unnecessary regulations affecting business, I believe we would have had what is considered full employment; the problem is 100's of billions of dollars left our country and went to countries like China and Mexico.

Present Trump is currently addressing this problem and the economy is booming and will only improve as he makes more changes to NAFTA and AFTA. He has already cancelled many of the regulations that were strangling business. When you look at these two issues coupled with the big tax break for business, you can see why the unemployment rate has plummeted.

Our government's policy of endorsing NAFTA and AFTA need to be rescinded and go back to a tariff structure where goods that are imported from third world; there I go again (I mean developing countries) and they are developing using our money, have a tariff added to keep American made goods competitive. The same tariff structure would apply to parts or any goods manufactured in foreign countries for US companies. This would mean that parts made in Mexico for the big three auto makers would cost the same as those manufactured in the United States.

Again, President Trump is already working with Mexico and Canada to make our trade deals fair and with China and Europe to do the same by placing tariffs on their goods to force them to renegotiate NAFTA.

You say. Wait a minute, wouldn't this raise the price on an auto; not if the ridiculous wages and benefits paid auto workers were reduced to reasonable levels; this is what the auto companies would be forced to do to compete. The wages would be less of a problem if tariffs were added along with a reasonable adjustment to union wages and benefits.

I have a theory about how American auto makers are trying to contain costs while refusing to fight these unions demands; they accomplish this in two ways; transfer the parts business out of the country and cheapen the quality of the parts. We the consumer ends up with poor quality autos.

The union is supposed to protect the jobs of their members but what has happened over the years is the unions desire to extort unreasonably high wages and benefits from the employer is the most important goal even if it means many of it's members losing their jobs when the parts manufacturing are outsourced to foreign countries.

I love statements by auto makers like number one in initial quality. Translation; when the auto is brand new it works fine because even cheap or poorly designed parts work for awhile, just wait.

My wife had a 2001 Jeep Grand Cherokee Limited with all the bells and whistles, what a lemon! This by far is the worse car I have ever owned. The power windows are operated by an assembly in the doors that consists of a tiny motor and nylon cord. I have had to replace three of the four window units at a cost of about $450 each. The parts can't be replaced individually but only as a whole assembly. The two rear windows are almost never operated as we have no children at home and both had to be replaced. When I went to the dealer for the part, it said "made in Mexico" When the heat and air quit working it was because a cheap little plastic door broke in the dash requiring the entire dash be removed at a cost of $20 part and $1000 labor.

The parts were cheap junk and the design had to be with the intention of making more money in repairs and parts than they made on the original sale of the car. If this is not the case Chrysler needs to hire new design engineers that know what there doing and quit using these poor quality parts.

This can only happen if our elected officials put a stop to NAFTA and AFTA or at least, renegotiate the trade deal and if this were to happen dozens of items we all purchase would be more expensive; this means we could buy less things, but we can't have our cake and eat it too (another old saying) What good to have cheap products if you don't have a job or a family member or friend is unemployed?

The bottom line is this; if those countries we buy so much from bought the same amount from us, everything would work out fine; let's apply a little common sense here; how do people making a fraction of the American wage afford to buy our products? All you have to do is look at the countries we import the most goods from and compare what they buy from us.

I don't believe most Americans think it is the United States responsibility to raise the standard of living of developing nations (I finally got it politically correct) at the expense of American jobs.

America needs to drop out of the United Nations as they have become so radicalized and anti American that there is no longer any advantage to the United States to be a member and as an extra bonus we no longer would pay 22 percent of the entire UN budget while the other 191 countries combined pay 78 percent; not only are we foolish enough to pay such an outlandish amount, but the UN almost never backs the United States. What was that famous old saying by P.T.Barnum (there's a sucker born every minute?) I believe the world in general views the United States as an easy mark and I have to quote another old saying at this point (if the shoe fits, wear it).

Another problem that President Trump is addressing and other countries have agreed to pay more; that helps financially but how do we get them to be more supportive of us?

Recently President Trump declared Jerusalem as the capital of Israel; the UN was not supportive at all as they lean most often towards the Muslims. The last three presidents all stated they were in favor of this but none of them did anything to make it happen. A typical case of sweet talk and no action. You now see signs carried by Trump supporters that say "promises made promises kept" what a delightful change.

The governments, State and Federal have way too many employees and they are paid far in excess of what they would earn for the same job in the free market; not only are they paid too much but the cost of their benefits also far exceeds those in the business world. Federal workers working at comparable jobs are paid 21 percent more per hour than the private sector and when you add the difference in the benefits they receive, the difference in pay is between 30 percent and 40 percent

Since Federal employees are paid from out taxes, does it seem fair that a worker in the private sector should be paying taxes so a person doing the same job in the government gets 30 percent to 40 percent more pay?

How much could the government (which is us) save if these workers were paid the same as the private sector considering there are 2.76 million employees on the Federal government payroll?

The same pay differential exists with the state workers when compared to the private sector. Using the State of North Carolina as an example; the State worker in pay and benefits makes 20% more than a comparable worker in the private sector. The State has over 170,000 full and part time workers. How can it be that a state that can't meet its budget pays its workers 20% more than it should?

Socialist programs at both the Federal and State levels must be cut drastically. Starting with President Johnson's 1964 "war on poverty", the amount of money that has been spent on social welfare programs in 2011 dollars is 15.1 trillion. Compare this to the 6.8 trillion to fund every war from the revolution through Afghanistan.

State social welfare programs account for about 283 billion while the Federal Government spent 746 billion or 21 percent of the total Federal outlay; that makes the total welfare spending for 2011 1.08 trillion dollars.

Public assistance programs account for 43 percent of all public aid spending and this is a 48 percent increase since 1980.

In the early days of our country there were no welfare programs; people were expected to work at what ever job they could find to support their family and now, we have created a freeloading society that are perfectly content to set home and collect food stamps, rent subsidy, aid to dependent children etc. This would have been considered a disgrace to have your friends and neighbors supporting you and your family.

Welfare needs to end and replaced with workfare. The states have cleanup of lakes and streams; along roadways and grass cutting. There are road repairs and countless other jobs that could be performed by those receiving public assistance. If they have children, the state needs to open day cares and use the people on assistance to watch them. The pay would be just enough to get by to encourage them to find jobs in the private sector.

President Trump recently issued an executive order instructing all departments to look for ways to reduce these expenses including giving the states more control over these programs including changing welfare to workfare; again President Trump is addressing most of the major issues that I am concerned with; this is indeed a president that walks the talk while most past presidents talked and campaigned about these problems but never did one thing to try and correct them.

The Federal and State government need to immediately establish a balanced budget (no more borrowing) and it doesn't matter how many programs or job cuts will be required. Both federal and state governments operate under the premises that borrowing instead of cost cutting during lean times is the way to go because as soon as things improve, they not only can stop borrowing but actually can pay back what they borrowed. The truth is it has never worked that way; even if on rare occasions they achieve a balanced budget as occurred twice under Bill Clinton; there was never any money to pay on the borrowed money from past years.

You and I as individuals, when we have overextended ourselves and no one will risk loaning us any more money, are forced to reduce our spending; in other words make sacrifices to get our finances back in order and hopefully we won't make the same mistake again but will get our spending habits under control.

The federal and state governments don't have the spending restrictions placed on them as individuals do because the individual makes a fixed income and has no why to increase it to cover additional spending; while the governments can just add or increase existing taxes to cover their spending habits.

A tiny light at the end of the tunnel is the Tea Party Movement; these are Americans that have come to realize they better do something now before it's too late. They have already influenced several elections in an attempt to get fiscal conservatives elected to congress. More Americans need to recognize how important this movement is and get involved In a recent vote Tea Party Representatives tried to stop or at least change Obama Care but the old established Republicans shot them down; I recently changed my political affiliation from Republican to unaffiliated because they talk a good story but always cave.

You and I are at fault for our governments runaway spending because we don't get involved in politics. As long as we have a job and are living comfortably, we don't seem to even care what our governments are doing.

We ought to care based on principle and moral values even when we are personally comfortable with our lifestyle.

By just complaining but doing nothing concerning our governments transgressions, we have arrived at a critical time in American history; both morally and financially. Maybe the reason we have arrived at this point is because the majority of Americans have become selfish, only caring for themselves or their immediate family. They do what they want without regard for morals, values or Godliness.

Healthcare

Neither the Democrat nor the Republican Parties have done anything to address the rising cost of Healthcare. The Bust Administration controlled both houses of Congress for eight years and failed to seriously address healthcare. The biggest single complaint I have with those eight years is the fact they accomplished so little.

If you are one to say but the Obama Administration had passed Healthcare reform, you would be absolutely correct; their reform however; is like out of the frying pan and into the fire (another old saying). What Obama has done to Healthcare is an attempt to convert our system into a Socialist Healthcare program. You don't have to be a political analyst to figure out that his main purpose was to provide free Healthcare for the poor mainly Black and Hispanic. When I said free, I am referring to the uninsured; it will not be free for the rest of us

President Trump and the congress when it passed the biggest tax cuts ever also repealed the individual mandate that required everyone to have health insurance or pay a fine each year. Which is a step in repealing Obama Care but now congress needs to repeal all of Obama Care and replace it with a better plan. If John McCain had voted with his party, Obama Care would be a thing of the past and it was a known fact that John hated Obama Care but he didn't like the procedure being used to replace it. I have a respect for John as a good American and a fine soldier who gave many years out of his life as a prisoner: however, I feel he was a much better soldier than a politician. If the bill to repeal Obama Care had passed and new healthcare legislation passed, perhaps the midterm elections would have had a different result. I can't help but believe that John McCain's vote to stop the repeal might have had more to do with his anger with President Trump than with procedure concerns.

The only attempt to control increased healthcare costs was an attempt for the government to take over Healthcare and set the amount that Doctors and Hospitals could charge the same rate as Medicare. If Obama were able to accomplish this, then we would be a Socialized system with degraded healthcare and six month wait for a hip replacement.

So how can we reduce Healthcare costs? The costs generally fall into one of three categories, Doctor, Hospital and Drugs.

Let's start with Doctors; some Doctors especially surgeons pay over one hundred thousand a year for insurance because America has become a Sue happy society looking for a way to get rich quick. The terrible part is that the people that set on the jury think the same way and award unbelievable amounts even to the point that often times the judge has to lower the settlement as excessive.

Now the Doctors don't pay the one hundred thousand dollars for insurance out of their pocket, we pay when we make an office visit and if we have insurance, the insurance company pays the Doctor but then charges a higher rate for their premiums. In the end, we pay for that insurance.

Our politicians, regardless of party, should set a reasonable cap on damages just as we have on disability insurance; you get so much for loss of a finger and more for a hand etc. Juries or Judges would only be responsible to determine if the Doctor or Hospital were at fault and no longer be involved in determining the amount of a settlement.

Once Tort reform had been approved, the insurance companies would be required to meet with the government to determine how much the rates the Doctors and Hospitals are charged can be reduced. Once this was determined, the Doctors and Hospitals would have to provide the government with figures showing how much they would lower their office or hospital visits because of lower insurance costs. This would prevent the insurance companies, Doctors and Hospitals from pocketing the extra savings instead of lowering individual Healthcare costs.

Another savings that would be quite large is to stop the un-necessary testing that is done not because the Doctor thinks it's necessary, but to avoid a lawsuit. Tort reform should include doing away with allowing lawsuits because a Doctor didn't have a particular test run. Some of these test cost five hundred to a thousand dollars.

If a Doctor or Hospital has been negligent and the results have seriously impacted a person life, the goal should not be to make that person wealthy but to prevent future occurrences. Large insurance settlements just raise premiums that are passed on to us.

A board made up of Doctors and laymen should review each charge of negligence to determine if negligence was really the cause or was it a normal mistake that humans from time to time will make. A Doctor that has been found negligent for a second or third time would lose their license to practice medicine.

Drug Companies appear to have such an influential lobby in Washington that nobody does anything to help lower drug cost with the exception of finally allowing people to buy their drugs from other countries; even then Washington stalled making this decision claiming the drugs might not be up to quality standards.

If Congress would investigate the Drug Companies and put a stop to practices that cost Americans, there is a potential for significant savings. American drug companies should not be allowed to sell drugs to another country either directly or indirectly at a price below what is paid in America.

Advertising by drug companies by one study estimates they spend almost twice as much on advertising as on development and research, wouldn't you like to save that money on the price of your prescriptions? I believe there are two problems with allowing drug companies to advertise prescription drugs; it adds to the cost and encourages drug use. Have you noticed how many of these ads end with a statement like "ask your Doctor if this drug is right for you"?

We must finally address the most sensitive subject, obesity. The latest statistics show that 35 percent of adult Americans are obese and another 33 percent are overweight and the cost to the Healthcare system is enormous. I believe the only way to encourage people to get their weight under control is through their pocketbook.

When I say the cost to the healthcare system is enormous, I need to restate that to the cost to all insured Americans is enormous. Those of us that are not obese pay for their extra Healthcare costs because like almost everything else in our country, people are not held accountable for their actions.

The one exception to the previous statement is life insurance. The insurance industry knows that the statistics show a smoker will live several years less than a non smoker so their life insurance rates are higher; this has been the case for decades.

Why is it when statistics now show that the impact of being overweight and especially obese is more devastating to a persons health than smoking of alcohol abuse, do the insurance companies not charge them more for their insurance which would then lower the cost for those not overweight?

I think if I were a smoker I would be tempted to take the insurance industry to court claiming discrimination for charging them more because of the impact of their smoking on life expectancy while not charging obese persons and their impact is even worse.

The politicians will not get involved because of a simple fact and it has nothing to do with what is right or what is fair; it has to do with getting elected or re-elected. If 77% of Americans are overweight or obese and a law was passed to hold them accountable financially, do you think they would get reelected? The politicians could have addressed this growing problem before the majority of Americans became overweight but they waited too long; remember my previous old saying about a stitch in time saves nine?

The insurance industry has the power to make this change because they don't rely on the people's vote and they need the insurance just as smokers pay higher life insurance premiums or not provide protection for their family.

We the people, like those involved in the Boston Tea Party need to demand from the insurance companies, a lower health insurance rate if we are not overweight or smoke. If they fail to respond we need to form a Tea Party of our own and take them to court.

We need to force people that act in an irresponsible manner that impacts our life, to be held accountable instead of allowing or in some case even forcing those attempting to do what is right to share the results with those that don't.

I will close this subject with the following statement, if you want to smoke or become obese, be my guest, and just don't expect me to help pay the bill for your bad decisions.

Education

The federal education department needs to be done away with; education is the responsibility of the individual states; if the schools are not performing as well as expected, the voters in that state can replace their elected representatives with someone who can address the problems. As it now stands, money from the taxpayers goes to the federal government to the education department where most of it is lost to salaries and bureaucracy; what's left, gets rebated to the states with all the federal strings attached. If the states don't allow the federal government to dictate policy and curriculum, then they don't get the federal money.

If the states got the money without it going first to the federal government, they would probably get twice the money to help fund their education needs and no federal big brother telling them how to educate their children.

While were on the subject of education let's talk about the quality not just the cost of the federal governments involvement.

The quality of education in the United States has been falling for decades in spite of programs like "no child left behind". All of these programs whether they are federal or state initiated are no more than a political attempt to convince the people that something is being done to address the problem.

Are you impressed when figures are released to show how certain schools have improved over the previous year when it's something like this; this years math scores have risen to 846 compared to last years score of 844; now I think of this improvement much like I would think of a performance raise in pay at a job paying $20 an hour of 5 cents while your boss touted how much better your life will be because of this increase. I don't think there are many people that would accept this raise as meaningful, so why would you accept that increase in math score any differently?

The simple truth is this; your children will only get a decent education in a private school. If you think this is not true, then why do almost all politicians send their children to private schools? You would think that since they always vote down vouchers where a parent could have the money a state spends per child on public education to help pay for tuition at a private school, they wouldn't send their children there. The politicians make enough money that they can afford to pay for private schools where the average person can't afford to pay for a public education that they are not going to use and at the same time, pay tuition at a private school.

The point is America, why are you not demanding a voucher system when you know how bad the public schools are? What happened to the Americans that threw the tea into the bay in Boston? That occurred because of taxation without representation while we have a more serious problem of a poor education with representation.

The argument of many politicians and educators is; vouchers would be the demise of public education; perhaps it would go the way of the dinosaur and rightly so if it fails to do the job and meet the needs of our society. Public education was exactly what a young country needed to get started but in recent years has degraded to the point that a public education in America no longer equips a person to compete in the free world.

The advantage a private school has over public education is they can set the standard for discipline which almost is non existent in public schools. They don't have to follow federal or state guidelines so instead of teaching students how to put a condom on a cucumber they can teach them how to read, write and do math. The schools don't have to curve grades because of poor performing students. If a student is a troublemaker or fails to apply themselves, the school can expel them. They can establish rules of conduct and demand the student abides by them; in other words, their schools can be like they were 50 years ago when students outperformed today's students in every area including conduct and manners.

There is another advantage to the private schools and that is, your children will not be brainwashed into thinking like the liberal establishment that currently runs the public education systems. You won't have teachers telling your children that your values are wrong and are based on old traditions and racist ways.

What about our colleges, do they produce graduates that can compete with other countries? Why do so many employers prefer to hire professionals from other countries over Americans? The sad truth is our universities are run like our primary schools. A college education is required for jobs that years ago a high school educated person would have been qualified to fill. We can't totally blame the colleges because I believe a large percentage of their incoming students possess an equivalent of a ninth or tenth grade education in the 1950's.

Many of the students don't really belong in college but should be attending a technical or trade school. Their reasons for attending college range from mom and dad want me to have a college education to all my friends are going. It's very rare to find a person working their way through college as they don't have to between mom and dad footing the bills and college loan programs. The nice thing about not having to work at a part time job is they have all that time to party and binge drink.

The small percentage of students that should be in college come out as doctors, lawyers, architects etc.: while the remainder graduate with a liberal arts degree or business administration and after four years of not earning an income and thousands of dollars invested, are working as an assistant manager in a retail store. The sad part is you almost have to have a college degree to get even the jobs that require little skill otherwise, you would be lucky if they could make change without some mechanical device to assist them. The education system has created this and the parents have gone along because it was easier for them.

It seems there is a bit of a push by the Trump administration to get more students to attend a trade school because that is where the jobs are. A TV program I was watching some time ago was covering this very issue; a business owner was being interviewed about his not finding welders he needed. He pointed to a young man he recently hired and told the interviewer he was paying him $80,000 a year. It's like that other saying" supply and demand" when the supply doesn't meet the demand, the wages go up. This businessman said he needed 80 more welders.

I have to tell about a situation I encountered about 20 years ago; a couple in our church had a son in his first year of college who lived off campus; it turned out he moved his girlfriend in and when his mother found out she was mad; not because as a Christian he was living in sin, but because she had stocked his freezer with steaks and he was sharing them with his girlfriend; would you consider this money over morality?

Illegal Immigration

Something needs to be done right away about the illegal immigrants crossing the border from Mexico and many other places; it's not only costing Americans jobs, but is sending billions of American dollars to their home countries which helps their economy while hurting ours.

It is probably true that there are some jobs available for workers from Central America and Mexico especially in agriculture; however, as I have already pointed out they are working in construction, landscaping any other areas that would be providing jobs for Americans. If there were not enough Americans to fill those jobs then Government I.D. cards could be issued for immigrants.

No one seems to want to take the Bull by the horns (another old saying) and resolve this problem in the only fair way. Amnesty must not be considered as this encourages illegal immigration and there are too many immigrants for the available jobs without putting Americans on unemployment or keeping them unemployed.

The government needs to require all immigrants to obtain an ID card for use as a work permit; in order to obtain the card, each person must provide fingerprints, DNA sample, have their picture on the ID and have gone through a background check. This ID must be carried at all times like a driver license and would be required to obtain a job. In order for an immigrant to obtain the card, he/she would have to have a job already committed by an employer. If an employer could not find a citizen for the job or preferred to hire an immigrant, he would have to provide a list of available jobs to the government. I would think each State Government could handle this better than the Federal Government.

Enforcement should be directed at the employers as it should have been all along. If an employer hires an immigrant they must pay them the same wages and benefits as an American citizen; this would keep employers from hiring immigrants instead of citizens because they can get cheap labor. The only reason to hire an immigrant over a citizen would be because they were better workers or no citizen wanted the job.

The employer would be required to withhold taxes and Social Security exactly like he would for a citizen. The fact that an immigrant would not qualify for Social Security or Medicare could not be considered as the programs need this money and there are many Americans that pay into Social Security and Medicare and die before they qualify.

Illegal Immigrants should not qualify for any aid programs because they are not US citizens which includes Medicaid, food stamps, aid to dependent children etc.

Employers that hire immigrants that do not possess a government ID card or does not provide them with identical pay and benefits would receive a fine that was so large that it would be impractical to do so. A second offense would shut there business down for 30 days. I believe under these rules, the number of immigrants working in this country would be reduced dramatically opening up job opportunities for Americans and keeping more dollars in our economy which will create more jobs.

President Trump has been trying to build a wall to protect our border and has had little support from his own party and absolutely zero from the Democrats. To encourage support for the wall, he might issue an executive order that huge fines would be levied against all employers who hired illegal immigrants and have ICE start going to all these businesses. While there at it, they might want to visit the homes of politicians and issue the same fines if they have nannies or maids that are illegal

If these steps were implemented, the immigrant problem would be resolved as far as jobs are concerned; the border must still be secured for safety issues and to prevent the drug traffic from Mexico. If the worker ID was required to work in the United States, there would be no reason to cross the border unless involved in illegal activities like drug smuggling.

If you want to stop the gangsters and drug dealers we must allow the border patrol to use deadly force otherwise they have little chance of controlling the situation If the wall was built, there would be very little confrontation with anyone. I believe it's better to shoot the drug dealers than to allow them to devastate the lives of thousands of people many of them children.

I want to point out again that forcing business to pay immigrants the same as citizens will cause a rise in prices but your friends and family might now be able to find work; make up your mind about what is the most important to you, saving a few dollars for yourself or helping your fellow Americans that are in desperate straits for need of work.

Terrorism

This subject is of greater concern than many Americans realize. We all know about the deaths of almost three thousand people in the World Trade Center and how horrific it was but the worse is yet to come!

Previously I stated that I believe the final battle as described in the bible will be religious not country against country and that I believe it will be the Muslims against the Christians and Jews. I also pointed out that Gaddafi former head of Libya has stated that Europe and America will have to become Muslim or declare war against them.

The discussion goes on and on in our country concerning the terrorists Muslims and the good Muslims who don't support terrorism; the question is this, if a religious war broke out between Muslims and Christians and Jews, how would the good Muslims as they are referred to, react? I think I have a pretty good idea.

If the United States keep allowing Muslims to immigrate, then Gaddafi may have been right. Now it sounds like I hate Muslims but that is not true; as a Christian I pity them for following a man from the 7th century that they convinced themselves was a spokesman for God, or Allah as they refer to God.

The real problem I have with Muslims that I don't have with say, Buddhists, is the radical ideas their religion fosters. The Buddhists don't care if you endorse their religion while the Muslim religion considers all religions that don't change to Islam as Infidels. The religion's goal is to require all people on earth to practice their religion. This is a religion that practices violence against people of their own religion. A woman caught in adultery might be stoned to death and women in general are treated as property.

There was a recent case where 17 year old Tanya Gupta a Muslim girl had converted to Christianity and ran away from home because she feared for her life. She believed her parents would kill her unless she converted back to Islam. There have been other instances where this has actually happened in the United States.

If it eventually happens that a great war as the Muslim Gaddafi predicted occurs in the United States, we will have many millions of followers of Islam to contend with not only from possible violence but they would be able to provide valuable information to our enemy who they follow. How big a problem could this be? It is estimated there are 3.1 million Muslims in the United States in 2015 and growing.

Europe has enormous problems with its Muslim population which is many times the Muslin population in the United States. Their problems cover everything from welfare to violence. France with a population of about 20% of the United States has a Muslim population of about 5 to 6 million. They have allowed the Muslims to become too large a force and should have stopped the immigration years ago.

The United States needs to learn from others mistakes and stop the growth of the Muslim population. I realize we would receive a lot of criticism for restricting their immigration but there is another old saying that should apply here (sticks and stones can break my bones, but names will never hurt me)

Even if we stop the Muslim immigration, we have enough Muslims already in the country and those people converting to Islam to continue to pose a serious threat. The government agencies responsible to keep Americans safe must have every possible tool available including monitoring of phone calls between anyone suspected of involvement with terrorism without requiring a court order to do so. Privacy is certainly important, but death even more so! This does not mean the government should be allowed to monitor all Americans that are not involved in terrorism as they have been caught doing.

Many will say, I think he is over reacting to the Muslim threat and there is no way the United States will restrict the Muslim immigration because we want to convince the world that we are the tolerant nice guys; and besides, we want the world to like us and approve of everything we do. I would respond to those critics with the following statement, you had better hope that I am wrong; otherwise, the price that America pays will be more than you ever imagined.

While were on the subject of the Muslin world and the threat it poses to non-Muslims, Iran has been in the limelight for a long time. Most of the world including Muslim countries, don't want to see Iran possess nuclear weapons. The United States and allies working with the UN (you know how I feel about the UN) have been using sanctions in an attempt to convince Iran to stop their nuclear program, all to no avail. The problem with sanctions is some countries don't participate and the sanctions are never tough enough to get the job done. Most experts agree that a blockade of gasoline to Iran would bring it to its knees because while they have oil, they don't have the refineries to convert it to gasoline. Their economy would grind to a halt. This sanction has never been approved and most likely never will be by the UN. I won't even discuss the latest agreement with Iran because they can't be trusted.

The Obama administration working with 5 other nations called the PF+1 agreed to a nuclear deal with Iran in exchange for a lifting of some sanctions and many in congress thought it was a terrible deal for the United States.

President Trump just backed out of the deal and imposed all of the sanctions as Iran is a major sponsor of terrorism in the Middle East and other Arab countries don't trust them. Remember when those 52 American embassy personal were held hostage by Iran and President Jimmy Carter tried to free them with a military operation that resulted in 8 military deaths and no hostages freed. Iran can't be trusted!

The United States should fully support Israel in destroying Iran's nuclear facilities regardless of the impact because having a nuclear Iran is a much worse option, and Israel if the United States will not support them, needs to go ahead without us before it's too late.

When Hitler started to invade Europe, I believe Roosevelt would have liked to get involved earlier to help stop him from his quest to take over the world but the American people were so weary from World War one that they would never have approved of early involvement hoping instead the United States wouldn't have to get involved again.

Well the truth was, the Allies did not defeat Germany and occupy the country following World War one like they did following World War two so failing to do the job right resulted in a war that killed many more people than the first war. If the politicians and the American people had faced the reality of Adolph Hitler, they would have taken steps earlier and there is no telling how many hundreds of thousands of lives, both military and civilian would have been saved. We need to learn from our mistakes and miscalculations when we look at the situation in Iran.

Social Security and Medicare

Of all the subjects that I talk about, this one appears to be the biggest disaster of them all; I say that because in my opinion, there is no way to fix it without unbelievable changes and huge tax increases.

If Social Security had been left in a trust fund as President Roosevelt set it up, there would be a ton of money in it and Washington wouldn't be languishing over what to do in the face of impending disaster.

Baby Boomers start drawing Social Security this year and keep increasing every year for the next decade or two. Where is the Federal Government going to get the money when they don't have enough money to pay their current budget without borrowing vast amounts of dollars?

There are only two choices to deal with the problem other then making people work until they die, cut benefits or raise taxes. Congress doesn't like any of their choices so they keep postponing making a decision; eventually they will be forced to decide and the longer they wait the worse it will be (remember the stitch in time saves nine)?

Medicare is in the same boat with Social Security because those Baby Boomers starting to draw Social Security at 65 will also go on Medicare; gee, I hope the Obama administration considered that when they planned to cut 500 billion from the program.

The only other way to try and shore up these systems is to do away with the Socialist part which provides widow benefits, college for the children, etc. and just keep the entitlement portion which is what the worker paid for every working year.

It would be the responsibility of the parents to buy insurance just like they did years ago to provide for the needs of the family should a parent die.

Medicaid should be done away with and each worker that does not have insurance either provided by their employer or themselves should be required to put an amount, say, 5 percent of their pay into a medical fund which they can't touch except to pay medical expenses. When they visit a Doctor or hospital, the fee would be deducted from their account. This would also keep people without insurance from going to the emergency room which costs many times more then the Doctor office because that cost would be coming out of their health account.

You can say how can the poor afford to have a health account and I would say that the poor are not as poor as many decades ago when there were no free programs and they survived. The poor today have televisions, cars go out to eat etc; it is the responsibility of all Americans regardless of their financial standing, to meet their own basic needs.

To support my claim I will tell you about a situation I found myself in a short time ago. In our bedroom we had a 23 inch television which worked just fine but we had recently switched to high definition with the satellite company so we replaced it with a 32 inch HD television.

I went to the local thrift shop for the poor and took some food items and other things along with the 23 inch TV. The man behind the desk told me to take all the items except the food and leave them outside until they could get to them. I pointed out it was supposed to rain and I had a 23 inch TV. He asks me what kind and I said it's just like the one you have only larger. I couldn't believe his response. We have to throw those in the dumpster because they only want flat screen TV. I said to the man, I thought these were poor people, do they require High Definition and 3D?

We have to stop trying to copy European Socialist programs and go back to the ideals and values that America was founded on or we will end up bankrupt and in a depression where everyone suffers.

401K and IRA

It is obvious that I don't favor much involvement by the Government either Federal, State or local in our private business and having said that, there are cases where the Government does need to takes steps for the general welfare of society as a whole.

When we talk about the grave financial situation we face due to excessive borrowing, Social Security, Medicaid and Medicare, we can't overlook the situation looming down the road for retirees.

The number of companies that offer conventional pension plans where when a person retires they receive a monthly pension check for life and the spouse must be covered by at least 50% is about 10 percent which means about 90 percent of retirees in the future will have to depend on their 401K or IRA to supplement their Social Security (assuming there is Social Security then).

A recent article by AARP stated that about 58% of retirees had spent all of their 401K/IRA within 5 years. This fact shows how many people are not good at handling their money; with a pension they didn't have to be but now they have access to their 401K/IRA pension fund and can blow the whole thing many years before end of life.

Is our society going to allow them to live at poverty levels because they spent all their savings too soon?

The very reason Social Security was started was to force people to save for their old age and perhaps the same reasoning should be applied to IRA/401K plans.

When you reach 70 & ½ you must start withdrawing from these plans based upon an actuary table so in theory, the day you die, the plan is empty. The Government of course, wants their taxes that you were allowed to forego until time to start withdrawing. There is nothing that says you can't withdraw all of the funds anytime after you reach 59 & ½.

For those that do not have a company pension, their withdrawals should be limited to the same amount they are required to withdraw and should not be able to start withdrawal until they retire to prevent them from draining there account and becoming a burden on society.

If we don't do this, it will just be another financial nail in the coffin. For those that might say you can't tell a person how to spend their 401K/IRA, I would again point out that the Government was able to force all of us to put a portion of out income back for Social Security and it is doled out just like a pension plan, as a monthly income.

An interesting note about a ROTH IRA which works differently from a regular IRA; A regular IRA allows you to avoid paying taxes on the money you place in the IRA each year and when you start withdrawing the funds they are taxable. A ROTH IRA you lose the benefit of making money on the deferred taxes but when you withdraw, its tax free.

Two people, one in a standard IRA and the other in a ROTH IRA investing for the same number of years in the same investments will have a different amount of money in their IRA. The ROTH IRA will have considerably less money because they had to pay the taxes up front and therefore, didn't have that money to invest but the less money will be tax free (maybe).

Two things to consider before investing in a ROTH IRA are your tax rates and the Government.

It is most likely that when you retire your tax rate will be less than when you worked and if so, the amount you pay in taxes on the standard IRA will be less than the taxes you deferred all those years. Another benefit of having to pay taxes on the standard IRA is you will be less likely to withdraw large amounts at a time as it will move you into a larger tax bracket and it may increase the tax on your Social Security.

How about the Government; they tell you that there will be no tax on the ROTH IRA, right? The Government may renege on that promise and I give you the following facts to support my claim.

The money taken out of your pay for Social Security is taxed even though you don't get the money but that's ok because like a ROTH IRA, when you start drawing benefits there not taxable, right? If Social Security benefits were taxed you would be taxed twice, once when you paid Social Security and again when you drew benefits.

Well it did start out to work like a ROTH IRA but when the Government needed the money they changed the rules and started taxing the benefits so why would you think the same thing won't happen to the ROTH IRA after all the Government is in even worse financial shape now.

Based on the history of Social Security, I would opt for the standard IRA and get the tax break now because a bird in the hand is worth two Government birds in the bush anytime.

Military

I served in the Marines from 1956 to 1960 when it was not an all volunteer Army. The pay for a sergeant (E4) was $157 a month plus a bunk in the barracks and their food.

The average sergeant today with three years of service makes $45,972 a year which includes pay, housing allowance etc. Once we converted to an all volunteer army the cost to sustain it went through the ceiling.

Many countries around the world require mandatory military service just as the United States did until 1973. Once we went to an all volunteer army the cost went up big time just like everything else the government adds or changes.

The savings would be significant if we adopted a program where following graduation from high school, a two year stint in the military would be mandatory. The pay would be far less than for a volunteer army and the military could still retain career soldiers at higher pay scales to be in charge of the two year recruits.

There are additional advantages in that a portion of their salary would be placed in a college fund for when their two year tour was up. They would now be able to pay their own college costs instead of government loans and grants which would save another large sum of money and they would have gained maturity and more capable of making a career choice.

Its not uncommon to find that many college bound students have no idea what they want to do to make a living so they spend at least the first year (or more) playing and partying and why not; either their parents are footing the bill or they may have taken student loans or a combination of both. The Government (us) is owed billions in unpaid student loans.

If a student had to pay for their college education from money taken out of their pay while serving mandatory military service, I believe they would be much more serious about getting their monies worth.

The two years of exposure to many different careers in the military would be very useful in determining what career they want to pursue and perhaps do away with the play time while they are trying to decide. Two years to mature could also make a difference.

We are constantly ripped off by providers of goods and services to the military (I use the term "we") because we are the government when it comes to the money they spend so when they are cheated, it is "we" that are cheated.

Now no one knows for sure how much we are cheated by military contractors but it runs in the billions of dollars; when they are caught which you know is only part of the time, they are fined but rarely sentenced to jail. The amount contractors are fined for fraud is a small fraction of the amount they defrauded us for so it will never end.

I have to discuss accountability again because if we don't hold people accountable for their actions, we will never fix the problems.

Contractors who defraud us should have to pay back every penny plus a huge fine and mandatory jail time and if we were to do this, fraud would virtually disappear.

Does it seem reasonable to you that a person that breaks into someone's house and steals a few thousand dollars worth of property should spend more time in jail than someone that effectively stole millions of dollars from the people?

White collar crime gets treated with kid gloves and "we the people" have allowed this by not getting involved and standing up demanding stiff punishment for these types of crimes.

Perhaps in our society we have seen the corruption, graft, and lack of accountability for so long that we have become apathetic so it just gets worse everyday and we may even start to think that everyone else does it so why not me. For those that have or are raising children, think of the times when you told them no they would respond "why not, all the other kids can"; I'm not sure we all outgrew that.

Government Interference

The government trying to run our lives has expanded under the Obama Administration like never before and it's even extended to the states and cities.

San Francisco politicians passed a law preventing McDonalds from including a toy in happy meals because of childhood obesity which should be handled by the parents.

The Obama Administration wanted a requirement by 2025 of 54.5 miles per gallon average for all cars and light trucks which will have to have a huge effect on the cost and size of the vehicles. When government forces the auto industry to attain ridiculous fuel economy, it affects our personal lives and standard of living; if we have to pay hundreds or even thousands more for a car to meet the government's standards, not ours, and then it has the same effect as the government raising your taxes. To meet these standards the card would have to be smaller and less safe. Statistics have shown for years that larger cars involved in accidents have fewer deaths.

This kind of involvement by government in both business and private lives just keeps expanding and this was a bad byproduct of the New Deal Programs started by Roosevelt. As I stated earlier, when you let the government get their foot in the door concerning your private lives, it really is opening Pandora's Box

Obama Administration passed legislation regulating credit cards and what kind of fees banks could charge for people that were late on their payment or charged over their credit limit. There were many good aspects to this legislation which forced the banks to be fair in their practices which they were not. This in my opinion was something the Government should oversee. The down side which the government should stay out of was the requirement that if a bank increased the interest rate of a cardholder because they paid late or went over their credit limit; they had to restore their old interest rate if they paid on time for six months. The individual banks should be able to decide if and when they restored their interest rate and if the individual was not satisfied with that, then they can change banks or credit cards. The government just can't seem to keep from over stepping what should be their authority.

Obesity is a major problem and costs many billions in health costs so not only the Federal Government but more then half the States want to pass legislation to limit sugar in foods or stop having soft drinks in schools and on and on goes the list. If a person accepts being obese, the only concern for the State and Federal Governments is the cost and the same is true for businesses. From the standpoint of persons that are not obese, we should not have to pay for the extra costs. Insurance both life and health should cost the obese more than others and the fact that the insurance companies don't do this, you have to know that when they price the policies, those that are not obese are paying for those that are.

Since the government felt it should force the banks to be fair, why shouldn't they force the insurance companies to be fair. The same is true for all you can eat restaurants. Obese people that fill their plates three times pay the same as a normal weight person so you know that the price of the buffet has to consider the average food consumed per person.

If the governments, both State and Federal, want to do something about obesity then force the businesses to charge a significant amount more for the obese in all areas where the cost to the business or government is higher because of their obesity.

My view of Government involvement is that it should be limited to those areas that impact the welfare of others in terms of financial cost or security and obesity impacts all of us financially.

The area where the government got involved that had devastating effects on the economy and individual lives is the housing fiasco. The government in its great wisdom decided that everyone should own a home even if they were high risk borrowers. We just can't get away from that socialist way of thinking where everyone is going to be equal in lifestyle and that is never going to happen, but the government just didn't believe that so they encouraged Fannie May and Freddie Mac which are Government Sponsored Enterprises, to expand home ownership among low income high risk borrowers. Under normal circumstances the banks would never consider loaning money to these sub prime borrowers as it would not reflect good banking judgment but pressure from Washington interfering in private business changed that; the result was a boom in house prices. When the sub prime high risk borrowers couldn't keep up their payments the market was flooded with foreclosures and home prices plummeted.

We the people need to rise up and demand that our elected representatives stay out of private lives and business policies; in other words, we need to force them to follow the Constitution which severely limits the role of Government in our lives.

Jobs

Vice President Joe Biden made a statement that the eight million jobs that were lost will probably never be recovered and I would had to agree with him even if President Obama would have liked to staple his mouth shut.

The reason I agreed with Biden is because the steps necessary to put our people back to work, no one from either party was actively pursuing and the reason I believe is because of votes needed for reelection or contributions needed from special interest groups required to run an effective campaign.

Restoring the balance of trade, requiring a tariff on parts made in foreign countries, and preventing business owners from hiring illegal immigrants would provide jobs for all Americans but to my knowledge no one was suggesting such programs for the reasons mentioned in the previous paragraph.

Many of you will remember the Presidential election of 1992 when Ross Perot talked about how NAFTA and AFTA would drain all of the manufacturing jobs from the United States. During the debate with Al Gore, Ross said "the first thing you will hear is a giant sucking sound and that will be all of our jobs going out of the country".

When you look at the statistics, Ross Perot was right on the money. It is estimated the United States has lost three million manufacturing jobs in the last 10 years alone.

President Trump is already addressing these problems and if congress won't provide the money to build the wall then attack the problem with the business and private individual that hire illegals.

Now I didn't vote for Ross Perot because of many of his other ideas and also I didn't feel he was qualified to be President but his following statements were on the money and you will notice none of them have come to bear.

> The budget should be balanced!!!!!! (Without borrowing 1.4 trillion?)

> The Treasury should be refilled. (Is this with freshly printed money?)

> The public debt should be reduced!!!!!! (Didn't we just increase the debt limit?)

> The arrogance of public officials should be controlled.
> (That will be the day)

Now the reason the other presidential contenders were not concerned about losing the manufacturing jobs was there contention that the employees would be retrained for higher paying jobs.

I remember those debates and at the time thought; you mean the man or woman that is putting power cords on toasters will now become rocket scientists or brain surgeons or maybe even run for Congress; but wait a minute, with congress having only a 10% approval rating, how could the average person do worse?

About 68 percent of all people have average IQ scores and manufacturing jobs are perfect for them and provide a decent income; I suspect that many of those that lost their manufacturing jobs are now working at Wal-Mart or McDonalds for far less than they were making.

Now many elected officials will tell you that many of those displaced from their manufacturing jobs are working in services and I would say to you that most of those jobs are taken by illegal immigrants.

If you eat at fast food restaurants you will notice how many workers are Mexican and the same is true at hotels. Construction Companies employ Mexican workers that don't speak English and have a foreman that can speak Spanish. Landscaping and yard work is the same way. The list goes on.

The services jobs I just mentioned don't pay what the lost manufacturing jobs did even if they employed American citizens so what are these services jobs that would replace the lost manufacturing jobs?

Another aspect of losing our manufacturing capability should be of major concern for America and that is defense.

Many historians cite manufacturing capability as the main reason the North defeated the South in the Civil War. The North had about 6 times the manufacturing capability as the South so the South had to turn to Europe for arms, ammunition and supplies; once the Union was able to blockade those supplies, the South was doomed to fail.

It's probably true that millions of American jobs were lost because companies outsourced part of their work to other countries and for several reasons:

> Government policies make it more profitable to manufacture overseas.

> The unions have driven up labor costs to unsustainable levels.

> The quality of work is better.

NAFTA & AFTA are government policies that have to be canceled and a tariff system reinstated to account for such low wages in some other countries that there is no way the United States can compete against. Many will say this is isolationism,

The president of France indirectly criticized President Trump for nationalism, putting our country first but I say it is common sense fairness unless we are willing for our people to work for wages below the minimum and thus live in abject poverty like many in the developing nations.

In China the average manufacturing wage is less than a dollar!

The tariff should not be set to adjust to union wage scales but reasonable manufacturing rates. With the cost of the product about the same for American and Foreign made products, the decision to buy would be based on design and quality. If the American worker wanted to keep his job then he better build a quality product. We can look back at the 1970's when the quality of the American made automobiles by the big 3 auto makers was terrible and the Toyota was introduced from Japan. The difference in quality between the American made and Japanese made automobiles was astounding. My daughter bought a Toyota for $3800 and sold it 2v 1/2 years later for $3400 and we had several people wanting to buy it.

When I talk about the unions and how they have contributed to a loss of American jobs, I speak with experience.

My father started with General Motors in 1928 working at Fisher Body in Flint Michigan and retired in 1968 after 40 years. My grandfather worked for Buick in Flint for 41 years from 1914 when they had wooden bodies until 1955. My uncle worked 43 years for Chevrolet. The three of them had a combined total of 124 years working for GM.

The union at GM was started in 1937 in a conflict between the workers and management often referred to as the "Battle of the Bulls". My father lived in the shop for about six weeks before the strike was settled. The working conditions were terrible and the workers at that time just wanted decent working conditions.

By the 1960's, my father's opinion of his union had changed and he said that the union was now more corrupt than the management had ever been and their demands were unreasonable and outrageous.

The union demanded wages and benefits far exceeding other manufacturing jobs and even worse, when a person came to work hung over, the foreman couldn't fire them because they would go to their committeeman who would then threaten to close the line down; the result was they kept their job and build poor quality cars.

Quality has now improved because of the competition from foreign auto makers.

200,000 union jobs in the auto industry have been lost since 2006 because of competition, economic conditions and outsourcing for lower costs.

I have found it so interesting to see that the only solution to creating millions of jobs that have been proposed by either the Democrats or Republicans is:

1. Cut regulations that hinder businesses.
2. Cut business tax rates so they will be more competitive with other countries.
3. Cut personal taxes so they will spend more.
4. Raise taxes on the rich so the government will have more money to squander.

I believe only a minimal or temporary improvement would occur from any of these proposals unless the two areas (free trade agreements and illegal immigrants) is fixed.

President Trump has accomplished the first three and discarded the forth as that would have the opposite effect. He has also started working on the free trade agreements and illegal immigrants but with great opposition from not only the congress but surprisingly from many of the American people.

Now many politicians talk about securing our borders which might stop more illegal immigrants from entering our country, but what does that do about the somewhere between twelve and fifteen million or more (no one knows for sure) and yes, not even your hairdresser, that are taking American jobs.

President Obama and others claimed the immigrants only work at jobs that Americans won't such as picking veggies in the field and that is so naïve it isn't worth discussing. There are jobs in the building trades, landscaping, and various service jobs that Americans would gladly take if the government would stop paying them for two or three years in unemployment benefits to stay home.

So why isn't any politician talking about this huge hit to unemployment? Votes, votes and of course there's votes.

The employers are the reason we have so many millions of illegal immigrants in our country; they are here for jobs and if the employers would refuse to hire them and hired American citizens instead, our unemployment rate would plummet big time.

The employers won't stop hiring illegal immigrants voluntarily because the workers do a good job and they pay them less so profits go up.

It will take strong government enforcement with huge penalties for employers that hire illegal immigrants to have the illegal's go back to their own country voluntarily. The only way that will happen is if we the people put pressure on our politicians to carry this out.

The bottom line is this; the employers won't stop employing illegal's because it's advantageous to them. (Money)

The politicians won't force the employers to hire American citizens because it's advantageous to them. (Votes) Not only the votes but many politicians hire illegals as maids and nannies. Many don't pay Social Security or taxes on their pay which is illegal.

Neither the employers nor the politicians are adversely affected by the illegal immigrants, but millions of unemployed Americans are and that's not counting the billions of dollars they send out of the country.

The only way this problem will get resolved is if we the people put so much pressure on our politicians that they are forced to stop the employment of illegal immigrants.

Illegal immigrants would still have many jobs available but would lose some to the American workers.

Public Office

When we see all of the problems that we face and possible solutions, why is it that nothing is ever done by our elected officials to resolve them?

You don't have to be rocket scientists to realize that as great as it is, Democracy has its flaws. The people get to select who they want to represent them and that is a big plus; the down side is the politician has to please people once they are elected or they won't get reelected. The special interest groups also carry a lot of influence over a politician not just for the voters they represent but the money they contribute.

A politician is now faced with a decision to either decide how to deal with the issues; do I make the decision based on what I believe is right for the country or what I think gives me the best chance of being reelected.

Lobbyists represent every aspect of American life from healthcare to unions and as of 2010 there were about 11,000 registered lobbyists in Washington and they have tremendous influence over elected officials, again because of the people they represent and the money for reelection that is contributed.

I'm not just picking on the Democrats when I use this example of influence that result in poor decisions by our elected officials but this is a no brainer; the unions lobbied the administration to pass a law that would prevent secret votes by employees when deciding whether or not to unionize. If this had passed congress, then every employee who voted against joining a union at their job would be aware that the people they worked with who wanted to unionize would now know how they voted.

It is interesting to see Michigan become a right to work state; the unions have devastated the state as Flint and Detroit look like war zones with boarded up businesses and homes. Detroit has lost half its population and is the largest city in America ever to declare bankruptcy.

Why would the administration ever consider such a law when all voting in elections is private and confidential? The union vote was instrumental in Obama's election not to mention the many millions they contributed to his campaign. This example shows how the desire to get reelected which requires both votes and money can result in politicians making bad decisions. Don't forget the idea that the various lobbyist and organizations will say to the politician "we helped you get elected, you owe us".

If we don't take steps to correct this problem, the decisions politicians make will never be what they should be and what's best for America.

The first step that must be taken is to outlaw lobbying by any person representing a group of people or organization of any kind; examples would be Medical groups, Insurance Industry, Unions, Corporations, Business organizations etc.

Individuals would always be able to write, Email, or call their elected representatives to express concerns or request they vote a certain way on an upcoming bill.

No organizations of any kind which include corporations and unions should be allowed to donate any money to help elect a politician, neither directly nor indirectly. All donations received by politicians or political organizations such as Democrat or Republican would have to come from individuals or funding from the government fund that currently exists.

Once the influence of powerful lobbies can no longer exists, the next step would help ensure that our politicians make their decisions based on what they believe is in the best interests of our country; term limit.

If a person could run for the House or Senate and serve a term of say eight years and not be eligible to run again period; which means if you served for eight years in the house you could not run for the senate and vice versa.

Elected officials would no longer require money for reelection or support from special interest groups making them free to vote for what was best for us and not their reelection.

A simplified method to recall an elected official should be established at the same time to prevent being stuck for eight years with a politician who didn't fulfill their promises or should be removed for conduct reasons which would make them accountable only to the people that elected them.

An additional benefit would be people running for office wouldn't be doing so because they could serve ten or twelve years and retire with more money than most people would after working forty years A small retirement could be provided but not anything like it is today. I believe that most that would run for an eight year tern would do so because they wanted to serve their country not themselves.

Morality

How will the country recover financially and morally if people continue to think like they do today; we won't, unless their thinking and conduct changes and this will only happen if they get back in the church and establish a relationship with God. The bible teaches us that we are all born with sin and anyone who has raised children can see the truth of this statement. A little three year old that took a cookie from the jar when previously being told not to will then lie to avoid punishment. This conduct was not learned, but inherent in the human soul.

The only way to truly control our sinful ways such as lying, selfishness, greed, jealousy, anger, resentment and lack of compassion just to name a few undesirable human traits, is through the power of the Holy Spirit. It's also helpful to be reminded during regular church attendance of our weaknesses so we can work on them.

I have already mentioned how church attendance is dwindling which doesn't look good for our chances to change peoples life for the better. It almost always seems like a person has to hit rock bottom where things look pretty hopeless before they turn to God; maybe that is about to happen, who knows, Only God?

Glen Beck had a very successful rally in Washington DC: the turnout was great and much too many people's surprise, the rally was not primarily political, but about God. From all I have heard from Glen's talking, it became obvious he is a man that believes that God is the answer to all our woes and he does his best to convey this message to his listeners. It isn't that God handles all of our problems but guides and directs our ways so that the results will be best for us.

One thing I really admire about Glen Beck is his hope that people will see the truth about our country's dilemma if they are just informed with the facts which is something he earnestly tries to do with each and every opportunity. Glen informs the people of what is happening in America is every aspect of life from politicians, courts, religion, finance and every thing he believes Americans should be concerned about in the hope they will rise up and demand change; not the kind Obama wanted, but change that will restore America to the kind of country it was many decades ago.

My motives in writing this book are much like Glen's except I'm not as optimistic as I see Glen Beck. I would love to believe that the majority of Americans would be willing to change their thinking and their lifestyles, but I find this hard to believe. There may be some who read this and it will have a positive impact in how they live their lives and for others provide a warning of what may possibly occur in the not too distant future so they might prepare as best we can.

There is one truth that makes it difficult to have real hope for meaningful change and that is we operate as a Democratic Republic which means, the majority rule. In order to effect change you have to convince the majority to demand proper action from their elected representatives and even more importantly, from themselves.

There is nothing in history that I have been able to find to indicate that a society has turned from its irresponsible and sinful ways except in the Old Testament section of the bible where God was dealing with the Jews but even then, they always returned to a way of living that was displeasing to God.

I hope that Glen's optimism turns out right and not my pessimism (that's not really true about my pessimism) Realism is when a person looks carefully at the facts and comes to a conclusion without concern for whether it is positive or negative while a pessimist sees it as negative no mater what the facts show.

The facts about our country change day by day and perhaps down the road the facts will start to change my mind and I can begin to have a more optimistic outlook for America, I hope and pray this is true.

THE END!

By: Douglas Dickenson
       (General) History

Citations

Chapter 1

Page 6 $7.90 per gallon
http://www.eia.gov/countries/prices/gasolinewithtax.cfm

Page 6   Finland has a 20 percent value tax
http://www.wikipedia.org/wiki/taxation_in_finland

Chapter 3

Page 11   Unemployment rate stood at 14.6 percent
http://www.infoplease.com/ipa/a0104719.html

Chapter 4

Page 15   Only 28 percent of the workforce were women
http://www.ushistory.councilforeconed.org

Page 15   In 2000 64 percent of women
http://www.bls.gov/cps/wlf-databook-2012.pdf page 78

Chapter 5

Page 18   In 1965 the gross revenue
http://www-03.ibm.com/ibm/history/year_1965.html

Chapter 6

Page 29   Most abortions are not for
http://www.operationrescue.org/about-abortion/abortions-in-america/

Chapter 7

Page 31   The original rate was
http://www.ssa.gov/history/internetmyths.html

Page 32   If you assume that a worker
http://www.ssa.gov/pubs/en-5-10070.pdf

Chapter 8

Page 35   Frank Page a former President
http://en.wikipedia.org/wiki/southern_baptist_convention

Page 41   The median income for a person
http://en.wikipedia.org/wikipersonal_income_in_the_united_states

Page 43   Tarleton State University in Texas
www.foxnewes.com/.../texas-town-cross-plays-gay-chri

Chapter 9

Page 46   Jim Jones religious leader
http://www.en.wikipedia.org/wiki/jim_jones

Page 46   David Koresh and the cult
http://en.wikipedia.org/wiki/david_koresh

Page 54   Average American savings account
http://www.statisticbrain.com/american-family-financial-statistics

Page 55   In 1959 about 18,500
http://heinlinebackup.com/hol-cgi-bin/get_pdf.cgi?handle=hein...8

Page 56   Only about 10 percent of companies
http://www.bls.gov/opud/ted/2013/ted_20130103.htm

page 56   Statistics show that 39.4 percent
http://www.creditdonkey.com/no-savings.html

Page 59   Poll that showed about 55 percent
http://www.nationalreview.com/campaign-spot/230874/55-percent-likely-voters-find-cocialist-accurate-label-obama

Page 59   In 1950 28 percent of Americans
http://www.csmonitor.com/2007/0416/p01s04-usec.html

Page 59   Today it's almost 50 percent
http://cnsnews.com/news/article/terence-p-jeffrey/census-49-americans-get-gov-t-benefits

Page 59   Average hourly compensation in Mexico
http://bls.gov/news.release/pdf/ichcc.pdf

Page 60   Dollars sent back to Mexico
http://pewhispanic.org/2013/11/15remittances-to-latin-america-recover-not-to-mexico/

Page 60   In 2013 China imported from the United States
http://www.census.gov/foreign-trade/balance/c5700.html/

Page 61   In 2009 the average hourly compensation in China
http://www.bls.gov/fls/china_method.pdf

Page 61   How well the United States fared with free trade
http://www.census.gov/foreigh-trade/balance/

Chapter 10

Page 70   The current population growth
http://cia.gov/library/publications/the-world-factbook/geos/us.html

Page 70   Our current population
http://www.census.gov/popclock/

Page 70   While about 70 Percent of out oil
http://americanenergy/independence.com/fuels.aspx

Page 70   In 2011 the United States got about 19 percent
http://en.wikipedia.org/wiki/nuclear_power_in_the_united_states

Page 79   Cap and trade bill which would place a tax
http://www.cbsnews.com/news/obama-admin-cap-and-trade-could-cost-families-1761-a-year/

Page 71   A recent poll finds that 73 percent
http://www.people-press.org/2013/10/18/trusr-in-government--nesra-record-low-but-most-federal-agencies-are-viewed-favorably/

Page 73   Gaddafi in 2006 stated
http://www.wnd.com/2006/05/35992/

page 74   When the census Bureau hired some 700,000
http://www.census.gov/2010 census recruiting hiring assessment.
pdf page v111

Page 77   There are about 50,000 new cases
http://www.cdc.gov/hiv/statistics/basics/ataglance.html

Page 77   It's reported that about 52 percent
http://www.cdc.gov/hiv/statistics/basics/ataglance.html

Page 77   More than 200,000 living with HIV
http://www.npr.org/templates/story/story.php?storyid=97315837

Chapter 11

Page 84   How many of the 2,700 teens in 2010
http://www.cdc.gov/motorvehiclesafety/teen drivers factsheet.html

Page 84   We no longer would pay 22 percent
http://cnsnews.com/news/article/us-taxpayers-will-continue-
pay-more-one-fifth-un-budg

Page 84   Federal workers working at comparable jobs
http://www.cbo.gov/publication/42921

Page 84   There are 2.7 million employees
http://www.opm.gov/policy-data-oversight/data-analysis-
documentation/federal-reports/historical-tables/
total-government-employment-since-1962/

Page 84   Starting with President Johnson's war on poverty
http://www.cato.org/sites/cato.org/files/pubs/pdf/pa694.pdf

Page 84   Compare this to the 6.8 trillion
https://www.fas.org/sgp/crs/natsec/rs22926.pdf

Page 84   State social welfare programs
http://www.budget.senate.gov/republican/public/index.cfm/files/
serve/?file_id=34919307-6286-47ab-b114-2fd5bcedfeb5

Page 87   Latest statistics show that 35 percent of Americans
http://www.cdc.gov/nchs/databriefs/db82.htm

Page 93   It is estimated there are 2.6 million
http://www.rcms2010.org/compare.php

Page 93   France with a population
http://en.wikipedia.org/wiki/islam_in_france

Page 96   The number of companies that offer
http://www.bls.gov/opub/ted/2013_20130103/ted_20130103.htm

Page 97   The average sergeant E-4 with 3 years
http://www.military.com/benefits/military-pay/military-enlisted-pay-
breakdown.html

Page 99   The Obama administration wants a requirement by 2025
http://search.whitehouse.gov/search?affiliate=wh&query=miles+per+
gallon&form_id=usa

Page 100   Vice Joe Biden made a statement that 8 million
http://www.cbsnews.com/news/biden-we-cant-recover-all-the-jobs-lost/

Page 101   About 68 percent of all people
http://en.wikipedia.org/wiki/IQ.classification